Moss and Moses have written a unique and c(
how parental behavior may promote or discourage self-confidence
and independence in children. They provide guidance on parenting
that is grounded in theory and research, and encourage readers to
reflect on the impact of their own parenting styles and actions.
Many down-to-earth and humorous anecdotes vividly illustrate how
to parent at each stage of development in order to raise independent,
self-confident kids. I wish I had read this book when my children
were young, but now I have a terrific resource to recommend.

—**Stewart Lipner, PhD,** Director of Psychological Services, The Zucker Hillside
Hospital, Long Island Jewish Medical Center, and North Shore University Hospital/
Manhasset, Glen Oaks, NY

Through questionnaires, examples of difficult parenting moments,
and sound advice, Moss and Moses help readers consider their
own style of parenting. They give clear recommendations about how
best to meet the most essential challenge of parenting—raising
independent, secure children.

—**Amy Raphael, PhD,** New York, NY

This book is bursting with practical advice and essential skill-building
activities for raising confident children. It will go a long way to calm
the anxieties of both new and seasoned parents. Moss and Moses
skillfully illustrate how to help children navigate the winding path of
successes and failures in a way that will ultimately lead to their
independence.

—**Robin A DeLuca-Acconi, LCSW, PhD,** Certified School Social Worker,
Adjunct Professor of Social Work, and coauthor of *School Made Easier: A Kid's Guide
to Study Strategies and Anxiety-Busting Tools*

Timely and invaluable, this book is a must-read toolkit for raising
confident and self-reliant children. As a parent, I recognized several
strategies that worked for me in raising two happy and successful
young adults—and a few I wish I had tried! As an educator, I applaud
Moss and Moses for including an entire chapter on executive
functioning skills. These skills, rather than intelligence or aptitude,
are what set successful students apart. If your child is struggling—
in school, or in life—this book could be the most important thing
you read this year.

—**Colonel (Retired) Albert M. Zaccor, MA,** High School History and
Civics Teacher, Bridgeport, VT

RAISING INDEPENDENT, SELF-CONFIDENT KIDS

RAISING INDEPENDENT, SELF-CONFIDENT KIDS
Nine Essential Skills to Teach Your Child or Teen

WENDY L. MOSS, PhD, and DONALD A. MOSES, MD

AMERICAN PSYCHOLOGICAL ASSOCIATION • *Washington, DC*

Published by
APA LifeTools
750 First Street, NE
Washington, DC 20002
www.apa.org

APA Order Department
P.O. Box 92984
Washington, DC 20090-2984
Phone: (800) 374-2721;
Direct: (202) 336-5510
Fax: (202) 336-5502;
TDD/TTY: (202) 336-6123
Online: www.apa.org/pubs/books
E-mail: order@apa.org

In the U.K., Europe, Africa, and the Middle East, copies may be ordered from
Eurospan Group
c/o Pegasus Drive
Stratton Business Park
Biggleswade Bedfordshire
SG18 8TQ United Kingdom
Phone: +44 (0) 1767 604972
Fax: +44 (0) 1767 601640
Online: https://www.eurospanbookstore.com/apa
E-mail: eurospan@turpin-distribution.com

Typeset in Sabon by Circle Graphics, Inc., Columbia, MD

Printer: Edwards Brothers, Inc., Ann Arbor, MI
Cover Designer: Naylor Design, Washington, DC

Library of Congress Cataloging-in-Publication Data

Names: Moss, Wendy (Wendy L.), author. | Moses, Donald A., author.
Title: Raising independent, self-confident kids : nine essential skills to
    teach your child or teen / Wendy L. Moss, PhD and Donald A. Moses, MD.
Description: Washington, DC : American Psychological Association, [2018] |
    Series: LifeTools | Includes bibliographical references and index.
Identifiers: LCCN 2017023395 | ISBN 9781433828256 | ISBN 1433828251
Subjects: LCSH: Self-reliance in children. | Self-confidence in children. |
    Parenting.
Classification: LCC BF723.S29 M67 2018 | DDC 649/.7—dc23 LC record available
at https://lccn.loc.gov/2017023395

British Library Cataloguing-in-Publication Data
A CIP record is available from the British Library.

Printed in the United States of America
First Edition

http://dx.doi.org/10.1037/0000067-000

10 9 8 7 6 5 4 3 2 1

CONTENTS

Introduction 3

Chapter 1. Raising Independent Children: Knowing
When to Step in and When to Guide From Afar 9

Chapter 2. Confidence: How to Build the Skills
(Not Just Bravado) 33

Chapter 3. Executive Functioning Skills: Teaching Your
Child to Manage Tasks Large and Small 57

Chapter 4. Decision Making: Tips for Helping Your
Child Make Healthy Choices 81

Chapter 5. Frustration Tolerance: Developing Your Child's
Patience and Ability to Manage Obstacles 101

Chapter 6. Self-Monitoring: Teaching Your Child
to Look Within 125

Chapter 7. Social Skills: Building Your Child's
Social Competence 151

Chapter 8.   Independent Technology Use: Teaching Children
About the Risks and Benefits   *179*

Chapter 9.   Raising Independent Children in Special
Circumstances   *209*

Conclusion   *231*

Suggested Readings   *239*

Index   *241*

About the Authors   *247*

RAISING INDEPENDENT,
SELF-CONFIDENT KIDS

INTRODUCTION

Parenting can be an enjoyable, rewarding, and special experience, yet often is filled with times of uncertainty, stress, and anxiety. When your child is a baby or toddler, you may ask in desperation, *When will she finally go to sleep?* When your child is in elementary school (or maybe even in middle and high school), you may wonder, *How much help should I offer him with his report?* When your child becomes a teen, you may think, *Should I encourage her to go for that summer job? Can I trust her to get herself to work on time when I'm not available to wake her up?* The questions never seem to end, even when your child launches into higher education, career, and even becomes a parent him- or herself.

Every day, every stage of your child's or teen's development brings unique challenges and, hopefully, wonderful times. In a variety of situations, many of us ask the same basic question over and over: *When do I step in, and when do I watch it play out?* It's a question, essentially, about independence. How much independence can your child handle? How much should you support and guide your child versus doing things for her or him?

Children and teens of all ages can learn skills that help them to be independent. This book is for expectant parents, foster and adoptive parents, parents of infants and toddlers, and parents of children in kindergarten through high school. The skills described in this book are meant to be adaptable to your child's age and unique personality and abilities. Although independence and autonomy are values in some ways entangled with culture, we believe that there are many ways to teach these skills that fit one's cultural values and beliefs. Children and teens from all cultures can benefit from learning the abilities that can lead to becoming a healthy, competent adult.

For young children, independence might look like picking up food with fingers or a fork to feed him- or herself, or it might look like putting away one toy before getting out a new one. For school-age kids, independence may mean starting homework at a consistent time without prompting. Or it could mean that your 11-year-old with diabetes speaks up for herself at school when she feels that her blood sugar is out of whack. Independence for a teen can look like "doing the right thing" when at a friend's house where drugs are available. Or it might involve your teen asking advice from you or from a teacher, neighbor, or other non-parent adult about topics for which the adult has a certain amount of expertise. For instance, a teen might ask her swim coach for advice about what to eat before a big swim meet.

Independence doesn't mean children do everything for themselves. It means knowing when they can and should do things by themselves, and when to ask others for help. An important part of becoming an adult, after all, is knowing when to turn to experts and when to be self-reliant.

As professionals who have worked with parents and families for many decades, we know that many parents struggle to teach their children to become self-sufficient and independent. Some parents struggle a great deal, whereas others seem to more effortlessly find the right path for each of their children. We hope to ease your parenting journey as you read the tips and advice within the pages of this book.

Through our clinical work, and informed by research in developmental psychology and psychiatry, we've refined some key strategies and techniques to help foster more independent children and grown-ups. We've learned from what children and teenagers have shared with us, and we wrote this book so you, the parent, can feel more comfortable raising confident kids who grow up to be independent adults.

As you read this book, you will get the opportunity to reflect on your parenting style as well as on the personality and abilities of your child. Each chapter begins with a survey about your approach to parenting. We invite you to revisit your responses after reading about each topic. The surveys pose "What would you do?" scenarios as you raise your children at different ages. If a scenario is about a child who is older than yours is currently, try to imagine how you might handle the situation in the future. For instance, if the scenario is about driving and your child has not reached driving age, this might be a great time to start to think about how you might parent later on. And we encourage you to think back on things you did or wish you had done better when your child was younger. If you're parenting a teen and worry that you missed teaching some of the early lessons of independence, there's no need to panic: Life offers many chances to try again. Remember, teenagers' bodies finish maturing before their brains do. There is still time to teach their brains new habits!

In Chapters 1 and 2 we define *independence* and offer some ways you can encourage autonomy during various developmental stages. We have found that as children grow from toddlers to adults, there are some key ingredients that help nurture independence. When children have true self-confidence, as opposed to bravado or low confidence, they may be more willing to take healthy and appropriate risks. Watching your child take risks may seem scary, but healthy risks are essential to growth. Children who are confident enough to take risks also, paradoxically, are frequently confident enough also to be able to accept guidance from trusted adults.

Chapter 3 is about teaching your child to organize responsibilities, prioritize and initiate tasks, and persevere as he or she works toward goals. These skills are part of a broader area of maturation and ability to handle assignments, work, and situations requiring executive functioning.

Many children make impulsive decisions based on their desires at a particular time. Does this describe your child? If so, you will learn some tips in Chapter 4 for supporting him as he makes thoughtful and productive decisions toward short-term as well as long-term goals.

Chapter 5 covers patience and frustration. We all feel frustrated at times. This does not necessarily differentiate a healthy and independent adult from one who struggles to make appropriate choices. However, the ability to handle frustration and be patient when needed is an important skill for success.

When children are capable of monitoring their own behavior and decisions, they are more prepared to be self-sufficient. See Chapter 6 for ways to foster this skill in your children.

Chapter 7 focuses on social competence and how to teach children and teenagers to understand and respond to social cues. We also talk about how their actions and reactions can affect their success with friends, teachers, acquaintances, and all those who they meet in society.

Our technologically sophisticated society has much to offer parents and children but is full of pitfalls and obstacles as well. Helping your child gain a healthy ability to navigate through the technology maze is essential. Chapter 8 explores this topic.

Finally, Chapter 9 discusses the special circumstances that some children may face (e.g., divorce, loss, shyness, learning disability, blended families) and how parents can use these experiences as learning opportunities to foster coping strategies and maturity.

Throughout the book, we offer case examples to highlight points made in the chapters. Most of these examples are compilations from the hundreds of parents and children whom we have supported over the years. Other examples are based on real people (whose identities have been disguised), to illustrate how you can teach independence skills to children and teens of different ages. We hope you see yourself and your child, past, present, or future, reflected in the scenarios. We also hope you can use the examples as models and jumping-off places for asking and sharing advice in conversation with other parents. As mentioned before, there are many right ways and endless variations for teaching the skills in this book.

We refer most often in this book to "your child," singular, knowing that you, and our other readers, have varying numbers of children. If you have more than one child in your life, we imagine one might have to learn social cues, whereas another might need more help in another area. Since no two children are identical, parenting is always an interesting adventure! Our idea is to help you to teach the skills in a way that's tailored to each child's age, personality, and traits.

CHAPTER I

RAISING INDEPENDENT CHILDREN: KNOWING WHEN TO STEP IN AND WHEN TO GUIDE FROM AFAR

Do you struggle with how much independence to give your child? If so, you are not alone. It's easy to know how much independence to give a newborn. Healthy newborns can independently do some basic life functions such as breathing, but they obviously can't feed or clothe themselves or take care of household responsibilities or hygiene. For young babies and children, sucking on a thumb or finding a favorite blanket, for example, is one of the first signs of independent self-soothing. By the toddler years, many children seek total independence for brief periods. Walking away from mommy and feeling proud of the ability to do so, but then quickly looking back to make sure mommy is still there, is a typical way young children briefly experiment with being on their own. There can be panic on the face of some toddlers if they can't find their parents after venturing off in moments of independent exploration. Have you ever had this reaction from your own child?

The balance, or dance, between seeking independence and wanting to be taken care of is something we all go through at various points in our life. Your challenge is to help your child become more and more capable of being independent, even if he sometimes prefers you to handle certain situations for him. With consistent encouragement, children can learn to persevere at a task that is reasonable and reachable for them, even if it requires several attempts before they master it. This process, however, requires some patience on your part because sometimes it's just quicker and easier to take care of a situation yourself.

Raising a child who becomes an independent adult is a long-term goal. A child doesn't become independent at a particular age. It's not like specific milestones such as toilet training or losing baby teeth. Developing skills of being independent is a process. The time frame is determined by your child's age, personality, and life experiences and by your guidance and modeling.

Before reading further in this chapter, take a minute to reflect on when you might allow (or even encourage) your child to independently handle tasks versus when you might step in and guide or even fully take care of the situation. If your child has already passed the age indicated in the item, reflect on how you handled the situation in the past. If your child has not yet reached the age indicated, imagine how you think you will handle the scenario, or what you hope you'll do. This quick exercise is not a test or a judgment on you as a parent. However, it may help you reflect on your style of parenting.

For each item listed below, fill in the number that corresponds best to your response:

I = *never,* 2 = *sometimes,* 3 = *often,* 4 = *very often,* 5 = *always.*

_____ If my child (age 10) confides in me that she is having a problem with a friend, I try to first hear her ideas for dealing with the issue, and then I may offer additional suggestions, but I prefer not to get directly involved by calling the other child's parent unless I view the situation as serious.

(continues)

_____ If my child is struggling with a school project, I tend to take over to fix it.

_____ I tend to overlook the fact that my child (age 12) doesn't do his chores because it's easier and faster for me to do them myself.

_____ I let my child (age 5) struggle a little bit when she is learning to tie her shoelaces because we practiced it and I think she is capable of doing it and will feel proud of her efforts.

_____ I feel comfortable taking over and handling situations that I know are beyond my child's current ability (e.g., he has tried to tell an older child to stop punching him, but he continues to get picked on).

_____ I feel comfortable allowing my responsible child (age 16) to take on an age-appropriate job after school and manage her own money.

EVERYONE TALKS ABOUT *INDEPENDENCE*, BUT WHAT IS IT?

Is it ever possible to be totally independent in life? To some degree, that depends on your definition of independence. How many people do you know who grow all their own fruits and vegetables, raise farm animals for meat, sew their own clothes, do their own electrical work and plumbing, fix their car when there is a problem, and so forth? There may be a few individuals who live this kind of life, but for most of us, it is okay (and even preferable) to sometimes depend on others.

For example, Eduardo, at the age of 20, was preparing to return home from school after completing his junior year of college. He wanted to leave the college town with a full tank of gas so that he wouldn't have to think about filling up during his journey home. Eduardo stopped at his regular local filling station only to find that they were out of gas. After a moment of annoyance, he drove to the next gas station and filled up. Getting out of town took a little longer than he'd planned, but he experienced no anxiety, no apprehension, and only a minimum of annoyance. Eduardo was depending on others to supply the gas he needed, but he was independent enough to figure out how to get his needs met long before the situation became an emergency.

Unfortunately, when George was driving across the United States, he realized he was low on gas while in the middle of a vast prairie. He spotted a gas station down the road and began to worry that he would not have enough gas to get there or that the station would be closed. George was dependent on this one gas station, and he was starting to panic. In life, when we are dependent on others with no backup plan, we can experience anxiety when that one plan doesn't work out or is not possible. This anxiety may even lead to a panic attack and a lingering fear of being on our own. When we have multiple options for how to resolve problems, there is often comfort in knowing that if one solution doesn't work out, there is another way to handle the situation and people to ask for guidance. Knowing when to ask for help and when to be self-reliant are two components of being an independent thinker.

Independence means

- feeling confident that you can take care of yourself or get your needs met with help from others;
- knowing your strengths and relying on yourself in these areas;
- knowing, and accepting, your weaknesses; and
- having confidence in your thoughts and opinions and knowing when to reconsider your view.

In addition, a child who is comfortable "thinking outside the box" can come up with creative but also realistic ideas and still know when to consult others. Such a child may become an independent adult who has a better chance of being an entrepreneur or complementing the existing approach of the company for whom he works. You have probably observed that there's a fine line between helping children learn to conform to certain conventions they need for simply managing the world and helping children find new or creative paths for their world.

Dependency, however, occurs when people first turn to others for help before deciding whether they have the skills to handle challenges on their own. People who do this may inaccurately believe that they can't handle new or difficult situations on their own, that they lack the courage or self-confidence to follow through on creative ideas they have, and that others will do a better job at dealing with the situation.

Of course, in some cultures, young people who are making decisions are expected to ask the opinion of elders so that their knowledge can be factored into the plans. This isn't a sign of dependency as much as respect and information gathering. The difference between acting appropriately in your cultural setting and acting out unhealthy dependence is whether you know you can do the task and meet with success. Dependence can be knowing that you can do the task but avoiding it because you don't want to feel the stress and anxiety of the attempt. It can also mean that you feel that you can't do the task and, therefore, you don't try and end up relying on others to do it for you.

People who are independent reflect on their skills, realize they need help in a particular area, and are capable of getting this appropriate support. As children seek independence, it can be helpful for them to know that it is a sign of courage to ask for help when it's needed. You can offer great examples by modeling how you manage obstacles, challenges, and your emotions during times of stress. You can do this throughout the life of your child (remember that parenting doesn't stop even when your child becomes a parent herself). By demonstrating independence and the ability to ask for help, you are setting an example for your child.

Throughout this book, we'll return to the theme of guiding your child toward doing some things for himself and toward accepting support when he needs it.

WHAT THE AWKWARD DANCE OF INDEPENDENCE LOOKS LIKE AT DIFFERENT STAGES

Through instinct combined with guidance, children usually develop many abilities to manage their wants and needs. Not all kids follow the same time frame, though. If you notice a large lag in your child's attainment of age-typical skills, get in touch with your pediatrician to see whether this is a concern or falls within the normal growth curve.

There are several different stages when children face the conflict between seeking independence and holding onto the comfort of dependence of earlier years.

The Toddler Years

By now you are probably well aware of the "terrible twos." At this age, a toddler learns the power of the word *NO*. You have to find that delicate balance between allowing your toddler to have his way and when his insistent decision has to be overruled. Clearly, any situation that would put the toddler in danger has to be overruled, for example, if he wants to run across the street.

Brady wanted to dress himself and kept saying "NO!" to each item his mom suggested he put on. He wanted to be independent and make his own decisions about what to wear. Brady's mom knew his preferences about clothes were not dangerous, although she preferred that he dress in a more conventional way with colors matching. After a few such exhausting battles, Brady's mom decided she would make a rule that would make mornings more harmonious and allow Brady to have some choices about his clothes. She allowed him to have "Fun-Dressing Saturdays" when he could wear outfits the way he chose as long as they covered his body and did not lead to harm (such as wearing his older brother's too-long pants in which Brady could trip and fall). When he refused to wear shoes outside on a Fun-Dressing Saturday, Brady's mom reserved the right to overrule him because going shoeless could lead to Brady hurting his feet or not being allowed into certain places. Brady's mother allowed him some independent decisions, but she had firm rules too, such as having him brush his teeth with help and offering only healthy food selections at mealtimes.

Dangerous situations aside, it's important to affirm your 2-year-old's "NO" from time to time, even though it's easy to get in the habit of overruling it. By doing this, you help your toddler build confidence, and you empower him to express opinions and be assertive. These skills are essential. After all, you want your child to learn he has the right to say no if a stranger asks his name or if an adult or another child intends to touch him inappropriately.

Along with a budding sense of control, curiosity for independent exploration also develops at the ages of 2 and 3. For example, Samantha ran from her mother in the department store to head for the toy section. A few minutes later, when she realized her mother was not behind her, she panicked and cried until her mother arrived. Samantha wanted to be independent and seek out her own goal, yet she also wanted to know her mother was nearby. This is an example of that awkward dance between seeking independence and wanting the comfort of being cared for and dependent.

What's confusing sometimes is that reactions that are appropriate for toddlers become inappropriate as your child gets older. Toddlers are still learning words to communicate their needs verbally, so when they want something they may point, gesture, grunt, say a word that doesn't entirely make sense, and may even finally cry, scream, or kick if they don't get what they want. It's harder for toddlers than for many older kids to slow down or stop the wave of anger or fear that washes over them when they're upset. When you're deciding on a strategy for helping your child calm down, consider factors such as her developmental stage plus specific strengths and/or challenges—such as whether she has a good vocabulary or has difficulty moving past sulking or pouting behaviors.

Imagine your child wants a toy in the toy store. Your toddler may try to take it and not have the language to express her desire for it to you. When met with frustration, your toddler may feel sadness, disappointment, or anger. However, your 7-year-old may ask for the toy rather than just reach for it. When her request is denied, she may be more capable of verbally sharing her feelings with you. You will likely have to respond differently to each child to help him calm down and accept your decision (or your compromise). Even though frustration that bubbles over into a tantrum is common for toddlers who are not able to get what they immediately seek, you still have to step in and comfort your child to minimize his or her extreme frustration.

Allowing your child to experience and overcome some frustration, yet also having opportunities for success and getting what she wants are both important learning opportunities for toddlers. Giving your child the chance to try a task that is within reach can lead to pride and a sense of accomplishment.

Let's go back to that morning routine. Say your 3-year-old wants to put on her own pants but is struggling. She may be able to hold her legs out straight as she sits on a chair, but when it comes to getting her feet all the way down through the holes, it's just not happening. Maybe the total goal of putting on pants is not within reach yet. Trying to attain a goal that is not within reach can lead to your child feeling defeated.

Sometimes there is a part of the goal a child can master. Can you let her sit in her chair and hold her legs out straight, while you help by holding the pants in the right position? Then she can insert her own feet and legs into each pant leg opening. She can feel proud of completing the task, even if it required some help to initiate. This is the delicate balance parents maintain when encouraging their toddler to accept help and also thrive on being independent.

If a toddler wants to be independent, he is seeking autonomy and may feel confident that the challenge is within his reach. However, toddlers often lack sophisticated judgment to know what is realistic to accomplish. Encouraging autonomy, yet giving your child realistic choices rather than total independence to do a task, may be the best way to offer guidance.

As toddlers grow into young children, it's helpful to frequently offer them choices so that they can begin to develop their decision-making skills. In the early years, you can offer your child two choices that are both acceptable to you. For instance, 6-year-old Courtney was offered two healthy options to put in her lunchbox for school: carrots or cherry tomatoes. Courtney felt happy that she was given this freedom, and her mother enjoyed watching her make her own decisions.

Early Adolescence

Independence is a process children are continually developing over time. However, during early adolescence (approximately ages 11–14 years), children often strive to take a big step toward increasing their level of autonomy. At this time, children try to figure out how to think, act, and react in a way that is true to their desires and convictions, while also trying to figure out how to keep accepting their parents' input and support. Young adolescents begin the gradual process of drifting away from dependency on their parents to seeking more time with their peer group.

Ava, for instance, was happy to go to sleep-away camp and experience some independence from her family and be able to make choices about new friends, which activities to sign up for, and so forth. However, she counted on her camp counselors to provide a general structure for each day. She was also glad to have letters from home, even though she sometimes laughed about her mom's advice to "check yourself for ticks!" Having some adult guidance and an occasional caring word from home helped Ava remain calm. On some level, Ava knew she didn't have to be totally self-reliant.

During early adolescence, some kids seem to swing wildly back and forth between independence and dependence. One day your child rejects you, preferring to be with friends. The next day, he is upset if you are not available immediately. For example, 12-year-old Patrick was out playing baseball with his friends. When his mother called him in for supper, he said, "Later, Mom. I'm in the middle of a game." However, the next day, he came home from school and found that no one was home. He frantically phoned his mother and father. His mother came home just 5 minutes after him (she was stuck in unexpected traffic). Patrick was relieved to see her. Even though he got along just fine the day before without a parent, Patrick still wanted to know his mother was there when he needed or wanted her to be available. When his parents later asked Patrick why he sounded so frantic when he called them earlier that day, he denied being frantic and casually said that he just wanted to know where his mother was.

As children transition to adolescence, parents also transition from raising young children to raising preteens who are branching out into the world on their own more and more. As your child seeks to be more independent, help him to understand financial responsibilities and how this can lead to more independence. Using an allowance as a teaching tool can often be useful so children learn to budget and save for what they want.

During this time of early adolescence, you have to be aware of the peer group that your child picks because this peer group can have a powerful effect on his value system and behaviors. In addition, although a toddler has to be protected from being overly frustrated, by early adolescence, this same child may have to be specifically taught to be able to tolerate increasing levels of frustration in school, in sports, and even in friendships.

In Chapter 5, you will read more about how important it is to let your child face struggles and frustrations, when you still should step in and help or guide, and why this balance is so important when raising a child to be an independent teen and adult.

Late Adolescence

Although young teenagers often struggle between wanting to be taken care of and realizing the need to achieve more independence, this conflict generally diminishes during the high school years. High school students usually have learned what adults and peers expect of them, that it's okay to ask for help at times, and they are becoming more aware of their strengths that they can explore more independently. Confident adolescents then focus on the rewards of accomplishing and excelling at one or more areas (e.g., academics, athletics, art).

Graduating from high school, in some cultures, may mean that children start to seek a physical separation from parents, such as by leaving to go to college. If this occurs, the separation and striving for independence may bring an acute resurgence of the struggle between seeking independence and simultaneously wanting to remain comfortable, "safe," and dependent. Whether the late adolescent is living at home or away, the teen's desire for increasing independence and a parent's desire to protect and care for that child may create tension for parents as well as children. Parents and older teens may engage each other in strong debates or arguments, stirring up powerful emotions. If you are at this stage now, it might seem like your teen simply discounts your advice and acts without even imagining the consequences. The turbulence might throw you sometimes, but in fact, this is a key stage for entering into adulthood.

On the day of Jenae's graduation from high school, she told her parents, "I decided I don't want to go to college. I want to go into the Air Force." She had told her friends about this decision earlier and liked the little surge of pride she got from their reactions, which were mostly positive: *Wow, good for you! I could never handle military life, but you'll kick butt!* Buoyed by her friends' surprise and encouragement, Jenae was hoping for a similar reaction from her parents. She still wanted their approval, after all. She was surprised when they reacted emotionally to her declaration and disapproved of the plan. Nevertheless, the three of them agreed to talk about it. Jenae was no longer a child, and she was considering some very adult decisions. Her parents were not antimilitary, but they had always envisioned their daughter going to college as the surest road to success. Jenae's parents explained that her timing was also not the best because she had already accepted an offer of admission to a college, been granted several loans and scholarships, and (thanks mostly to her parents) put down a sizeable deposit for student housing. Jenae acknowledged this but maintained her stance.

Ultimately, Jenae and her parents made a list of pros and cons for her two options. They also tried to find a compromise. Jenae was still upset at the beginning of their discussion, but when she saw that her parents were prepared to take her military ambitions seriously, she became calm and reflective. She realized her parents were trying to guide and not command her. Eventually, Jenae decided that her parents made some good points, most notably that if she delayed going into the Air Force for the upcoming year, the option to enlist would still be available to her. She ended up revising her plan and was willing to go to college for the first year. She would then think about the possibility of entering the service if she still felt strongly about it.

In this stage, teens usually respond best to parents who practice

- guiding rather than telling,
- compromising rather than winning,
- respecting their child's independent views,
- modeling ways to respectfully listen and then disagree with a point of view, and
- restating what their child said before adding comments so their child truly knows that his point of view and rationale were heard.

Of course, doing all this while still wanting to protect your child can sometimes be tricky and even feel risky and uncomfortable for parents. Remember those days when she was an infant, and you called all the shots to keep her safe? Those were the glory days! They were the start of the wonderful journey. Seeing your child become more and more independent is truly part of the glory days as well!

During this stage of late adolescence, you may be able to enjoy supporting your growing child's decision making, and you can begin to take on the role of guide. However, because it's likely you don't always know what your teenager is doing, this is not a time to assume that your child will independently make healthy choices 100% of the time. Communicating with other parents, making sure that adults are present at parties, driving kids and listening to the backseat conversations, and so forth, are good ways to keep updated on what's happening in your child's life.

If you learn that your child is about to make a truly dangerous decision, or you learn that he is involved with unhealthy activities, this is the time you should assertively and quickly step in, despite the potential outrage from your teenager. If this occurs, try to help him hear that you are stepping in because you fear for his safety, not because you enjoy meddling!

Early Adulthood

You might think you can relax once your child reaches early adulthood, especially if he has cleared significant hurdles such as graduating from college, being admitted to graduate school, or entering a career-track job. Even if your young adult child is in a committed relationship or is about to be a parent himself, this is an important time when parents can still be guides.

Being on the verge of total independence can be a frightening time for anyone. Your young adult may feel that he or she is sailing in uncharted waters. The confidence she had at age 18 may be hard to muster now; at the time when she is expected to be a self-sufficient adult, she may feel that this is a daunting task. Even though she's adept at using online videos to walk herself through simple repairs, learn recipes for cooking, and the like, it may take her some time to realize that even self-sufficient adults have to rely on others at times, and it is okay to do so. A video can't teach her how to feel safe again in the unexpected (and hopefully unusual) event of an apartment break-in, for example, even though she followed the checklists she found online for canceling the credit cards that were stolen, changing passwords, and locking her phone. These tools don't supply the young adult with the emotional and practical support that might be wanted from you and other confidants.

As you read earlier, even adults cannot usually do all things on their own—for instance, fixing the car, performing an appendectomy, or piloting the plane to a vacation spot. Some adults can do some things, and others can do other things, which is why it's the wise young adult who can pick the areas in which to rely on oneself and when it's better to rely on someone else who has a particular area of expertise. This is an important lesson to teach children so they don't feel the burden of having to solve all difficulties on their own.

This stage is tricky because you don't always have a clear direction for how much to take over and handle things versus how much to let your grown child handle things independently. In addition, there is the reality factor. Some young adults need to remain in the family home or receive some financial help due to unemployment or low income. At these times, you and your young adult child may benefit from sitting down and even creating a contract for how much financial support you will give and how your child will move toward financial independence. Sometimes, consulting a financial counselor may give your child more tools to achieve this goal.

When your child is a young adult,

- try to focus on giving guidance, not directives;
- be there when your child reaches out to you, but give him space and allow him to navigate through some situations alone (when safety is not a paramount concern);
- do not necessarily agree with all of your child's decisions, but remember she is trying to be her own version of a grown-up and may resent your disapproval or doubts;
- speak up if you feel that there is danger in your child's decision or path, but do so gingerly without appearing to criticize.

HOW TO GUIDE WITH QUESTIONS

From the time children are very young through their adult years, they are exploring and trying to understand the world. With children of any age, parents can often find themselves slipping into "instructional mode." Instructions can build up independence when, for example, a young child has to learn how to tie his own shoes, or an adult child is preparing to take over the car insurance payments. However, your child may start to tune you out if this instructional mode is your consistent way of parenting, especially as she heads toward the teen years.

When children are seeking help with learning a specific skill, this is often the time they are most receptive to the instruction. However, frequently, these same children may resist listening to you when they feel they have their own way to handle a situation. At these times, instead of telling or instructing, parents are often better received and heard when they guide their children to use their own decision-making skills. Open-ended questions can help here. When you pose an open-ended question, your child is more likely to sense your respect for his thinking skills and your interest in what is going on in his life.

Believe it or not, you do not have to wait for your child to grow up before you start having a real dialogue. If your child is a teen or young adult now, and you were not in the habit of having dialogues before, starting now might be confusing; still, it's okay to try a new pattern and acknowledge to your child that this is what you are doing.

The following are a few open-ended questions you can ask as your child explores independence:

- "How can I help with your project, and what would you rather do on your own?"
- "What is your goal in this situation?"
- If your child takes on a challenge and succeeds, you can say, "How does it feel to take on a challenge and accomplish it?"
- If your child takes on a challenge and tries hard but does not succeed, you may want to first congratulate her for taking on the task and trying to master it. Then ask, "Where can you get help so you have more skills to meet this challenge next time?"

CAN YOU SUPPORT WITHOUT "DOING"?

Sometimes, supporting means you are doing a lot for your child. Supporting an infant's healthy development is a lot of work as you feed, clothe, and nurture him. Even when your child is old enough for elementary school, you're still the one going out for the school supplies he needs, helping him to develop study strategies, and teaching ways to negotiate friendships. You may wonder how allowing your child to depend on you can lead her to become more independent as an adult. In fact, when children and adults know there is someone who can be relied on to help them out if they need it, they generally develop a sense of security and are, therefore, more likely to take healthy risks.

Becky, age 9, wanted to learn to ski during the family vacation. She was initially frightened at the idea of sliding down a mountain and maybe crashing into a tree. Her father assured her that he would first enroll her in ski school to learn basic skills. After she had learned and practiced these skills on a gentle hill, she could then ski right behind him down the slope until she was confident to ski more independently. Just before going down the first slope, Becky explained to her mother, "I'm a little nervous but more excited. I know Dad will be there if I need him, so I'm okay with going and trying."

As was the case with Becky, many people venture to try new experiences only when they are assured they are safe and have others to guide them. It is best, for instance, to learn to become an electrician, a plumber, or more commonly, to drive a car by having someone else to lean on during the initial period of learning. Knowing when to ask for help or depend on another person is a sign of independence. This is an important discussion to have with your child. Perhaps you could even point out when you rely on others and feel confident that you made the right decision.

"I'm here for you" is an important message for both young and older children to hear. However, this statement does not mean

"I will do everything for you." Saying "I'm here for you" means you're expressing love, support, and caring. When it's combined with your show of confidence that you know your child can take on some tasks entirely on her own, seek out guidance at other times, and know that you are there to help her if she is overwhelmed or unable to master a difficulty, the message is even more powerful.

The following are some tips for supporting your child as he takes healthy risks:

- If your child takes on part of a task independently or is specific about the kind of help needed, take time to acknowledge those efforts (e.g., "Don't you feel good about facing this challenge and knowing when to get some support?").
- Praising your child's attempts is as important as praising your child's achievements.
- Be careful not to judge or criticize but rather ask questions if you are unsure of your child's plan (e.g., "Can you share your thoughts about how your plan will lead to your goal?").
- With older children, it may be helpful to ask permission to add your comments so that your advice is not immediately rejected or seen as a sign that you don't trust your child's abilities.

Why False Independence (Pseudoindependence) Can Be Destructive

Independent children do not generally shy away from taking on new and reachable challenges. They often feel a sense of excitement about working toward and then accomplishing their goals. Knowing that they can get support if they run into an obstacle can help them feel secure as they strive to explore new challenges and endeavors. But some children develop only a false independence, or what we'll call *pseudoindependence*.

A child who has pseudoindependence works hard to build up a facade of confidence. He may feel that asking for help is a sign of failure, or he may feel anxiety about admitting he is fearful about a new experience. He might fear that help will not be available or that he will be judged negatively for needing the support. He may also fear that others will be critical of him if he doesn't act brave.

When this happens, children can deprive themselves of the chance to learn a new way to approach a task or a new way to cope with a dilemma. If allowed to do so, they may avoid important tasks rather than face their fear of doing it wrong or failing. That pattern of avoiding tasks can then persist into the future and have consequences. For instance, when it's time for a young adult to start looking for a job, she may be overwhelmed with anxiety, not feel comfortable asking for help or facing this fear, and avoid sending out applications. If, however, this same young adult had learned to face new experiences, confidently accept guidance, and know that it's okay to make mistakes while learning, the new situation may have been far less stressful.

Unfortunately, if your child is developing pseudoindependence, you may not even recognize it right away. He might be acting the role of being confidently independent while always secretly doubting himself. He doesn't share his doubts with you, maybe because he thinks you will just laugh them off. He might not feel comfortable admitting he needs help because he has never seen his parents ask for or accept help.

Teo, age 8, is always admired by his parents' friends for being "so independent for his age!" Teo saw his parents smile when they heard these comments. He felt, inaccurately, that his parents were so proud of his independence that he thought that asking for help would disappoint them. Over the next few years, Teo developed anxiety and stomachaches. He felt alone because of his discomfort with asking for help, even in school with his schoolwork. On the

27

surface, Teo continued to maintain his facade of confidence and independence.

Other children may try to act older to keep up with and emulate older siblings, appear to be the leader of the "alpha group" in school, or cultivate an image that would be shattered if they appeared "weak" by asking for help. In the worst case scenario, in their teen years, these children may switch their dependency to unhealthy supports, such as using drugs to alleviate their anxiety and/or choosing a peer group that makes no demands on them for academic, athletic, or other goal-oriented success.

The Lure of Helicopter Parenting

Wouldn't we all like to be dependent in some way? Imagine winning the lottery and being able to depend on your bank account rather than having to work every day for money. Many people love going on vacation at resorts because all their needs are taken care of, and they can simply relax and enjoy the pampering. If your child wants to be pampered too, that would certainly be understandable—right?

Having an infant to nurture and protect makes most parents feel gratification and a sense of purpose. It's normal to have mixed feelings (e.g., gratification and a simultaneous sense of loss) as your child grows and no longer needs the same amount of parental involvement. You might even be sad to realize you don't know all your child's classmates or about all his daily school experiences. The intense intimacy with your little one is no longer there, although other connections emerge as your child begins to share more opinions, feelings, and plans.

Some parents also find it difficult to let go, so they hover in an attempt to protect their child. We call this *helicopter parenting*. When the parent feels the need to hover, a child can draw the conclusion that he or she is not competent to be independent.

The following are some ways to avoid helicoptering:

- No two children are alike, so use judgment as to when support is necessary and when your child should be encouraged to handle the situation independently.
- Doing something for your child that she can do herself might feel good for both you and her at the moment, but remember not to deprive her of the chance for pride and confidence that comes from her hard work and achievements.
- When you feel a strong urge to swoop in, ask yourself, "Am I prepared to take care of my child for the rest of his life?" A child who never gets to take healthy risks is a child who never learns independence.
- When the urge to help too much is strong, ask yourself whether you are prepared to deny yourself the joy of watching your child become increasingly self-reliant.

These tips are not meant to discourage you from guiding, supporting, and having a close connection with your child. However, overprotection, coddling, or accidentally leading him to feel he can never handle the situation without your guidance can become problematic. Many times, a parent has the wisdom and experience to handle things quicker or better, but this has to be balanced with giving your child the chance to learn to fly solo.

STARTING A CONVERSATION ABOUT INDEPENDENCE

At the beginning of this chapter, you had the opportunity to think about and answer some questions about your parenting style. Now, after reading the chapter, you may want to look at the questions again and think about whether you still have the same answers.

If you are interested in learning how your child views her own preferences as far as being dependent or independent, you can ask her to answer the following questions. These conversation starters work best for children age 8 and older.

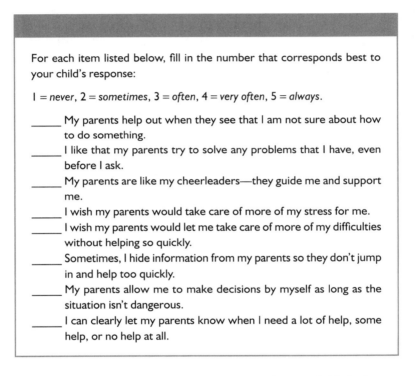

For each item listed below, fill in the number that corresponds best to your child's response:

1 = *never*, 2 = *sometimes*, 3 = *often*, 4 = *very often*, 5 = *always*.

_____ My parents help out when they see that I am not sure about how to do something.

_____ I like that my parents try to solve any problems that I have, even before I ask.

_____ My parents are like my cheerleaders—they guide me and support me.

_____ I wish my parents would take care of more of my stress for me.

_____ I wish my parents would let me take care of more of my difficulties without helping so quickly.

_____ Sometimes, I hide information from my parents so they don't jump in and help too quickly.

_____ My parents allow me to make decisions by myself as long as the situation isn't dangerous.

_____ I can clearly let my parents know when I need a lot of help, some help, or no help at all.

If you decide to try the questionnaire with your child, find some time afterward when you can listen to her thoughts without being distracted. When you do talk with your child about her responses, it's extremely helpful to show interest and avoid seeming critical. When she shares feelings about this delicate topic, it's like a gift. Thank her, and appreciate the trust given to you. If she is open to the discussion, try sharing your responses in a nonjudgmental manner.

During this discussion, you can talk about how she feels you can support her as she builds skills for independence.

WHY YOU SHOULD ALLOW YOUR CHILD TO STRUGGLE

Each stage of development leads to new explorations—and new cans of worms. Just when you think you've mastered the skills you need to raise your child, he grows and changes, and now you need a whole new set of tools to keep up. This is part of the anxiety and the enjoyment of being a parent. It's exciting to realize your child is changing and maturing! And adopting a parenting philosophy oriented toward independence can help you make consistent choices and feel less stressed throughout the journey.

Despite the fact that it can be difficult to watch children struggling with tasks, it's important for them to have the experience of struggling through age-appropriate tasks that are within their reach to accomplish. When children master challenges, they often experience excitement and pride, and they learn that they can continue to learn new skills in the future.

A Zen Buddhist parable can highlight the importance and benefits of the struggle. As the story goes, an older and a younger monk were walking together along a dusty path when the younger one spotted a butterfly struggling to emerge from its cocoon. This younger monk said to his companion, "It is a shame to watch the butterfly struggling so desperately to free itself from the cocoon." With that, he went over to the cocoon and started to open it to allow the butterfly to come out. He expected the butterfly to fly away. Instead, the butterfly fell to the ground, became covered with dust, frantically flapped its wings, and died.

Perplexed, the younger monk turned to his mentor and asked, "What happened?" The older man said, "It is during the struggle of the butterfly to emerge from the cocoon that it flaps its wings, dries off the moisture from the cocoon, and its dried wings become light enough to allow it to fly away." The younger monk realized that he stepped in to help but, in this effort, he kept the butterfly from drying off its wings to be able to fly.

Like the butterfly, children benefit from struggling to emerge from the "cocoon" of dependency to fly on their own. Like the young monk, you may feel the urge to step in and help. After all, isn't that what parents are supposed to do? When you're tempted to step in and alleviate your child's struggles, remember this story. Are you helping because it's just easier and quicker to do so or because the struggle is truly beyond your child's reach?

SUMMARY

This chapter stressed the importance of fostering true independence. It also highlighted the risks involved when your child acts out of pseudo-, or superficial, independence. In the next chapters, you will learn how to help your child gain the confidence to navigate through many trials and tribulations of growing up.

CHAPTER 2

CONFIDENCE: HOW TO BUILD THE SKILLS (NOT JUST BRAVADO)

If you think back to when you were a child or a teenager, you can probably remember some times when you felt confident and other times when you felt self-doubt. Confidence is not an all-or-nothing characteristic. However, as you will soon read, and as you may already know, a child who is confident can have an easier time coping with life's challenges.

Confidence can be impacted negatively by simply inserting an apostrophe *t* ('t). It makes the difference between the phrase *I can* and *I can't*. Have you ever heard Watty Piper's story of *The Little Engine That Could*? The engine's famous line was "I think I can, I think I can, I think I can." Who would have been interested in the book if all he said was, "I think I can't, I think I can't, I think I can't"? With a lack of confidence, the little engine probably would not have made it up the hill. The apostrophe *t* is often used by a child who feels he will not be able to do something. A child may convince himself that he won't be able to take on a challenge or complete a task well. Ironically, if you get rid of the apostrophe *t* from *won't* the child has already *won* (the letters left in the word)! When we open the door to the possibility of success, there is the potential for growth, regardless of whether we meet the original goal.

Of course, if a child feels he can do everything, despite the reality of his age or developmental level, this is not true confidence. True confidence is evident when you can realistically assess your ability to handle a challenge and when you understand when a task requires more time, more skill, or support from others. When you feel confident, you believe your goals are attainable, so you're more motivated to work toward them.

Before reading further in this chapter, take a minute to reflect on how you foster confidence in your child and your perceptions of whether your child is truly confident.

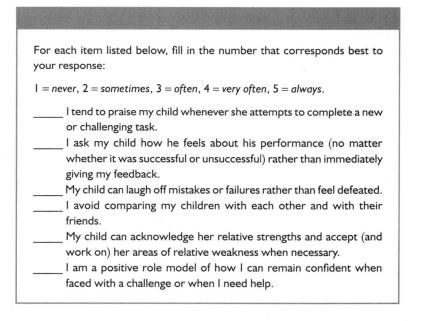

For each item listed below, fill in the number that corresponds best to your response:

1 = *never*, 2 = *sometimes*, 3 = *often*, 4 = *very often*, 5 = *always*.

_____ I tend to praise my child whenever she attempts to complete a new or challenging task.

_____ I ask my child how he feels about his performance (no matter whether it was successful or unsuccessful) rather than immediately giving my feedback.

_____ My child can laugh off mistakes or failures rather than feel defeated.

_____ I avoid comparing my children with each other and with their friends.

_____ My child can acknowledge her relative strengths and accept (and work on) her areas of relative weakness when necessary.

_____ I am a positive role model of how I can remain confident when faced with a challenge or when I need help.

Throughout this chapter, you will get the opportunity to reflect on how you encourage confidence in your child. At this point, however, let's review the different forms of confidence.

CONFIDENCE DOESN'T MEAN BEING GOOD AT EVERYTHING

In the last chapter, you read that a person does not have to be entirely self-reliant to be considered an independent person. Similarly, people can feel confident even though they are not skilled in all areas of their life. Would you expect a neurosurgeon to fix your car's engine? Would you expect your mechanic to operate on your brain? Probably not! Should the neurosurgeon feel less confident because her skills are not globally exceptional? Should the mechanic feel disappointed that he can't do surgery on a person the way he can operate on a car? The answer, again (hopefully), is NO!

It is less obvious to children and teens that they can feel confident without having the same talents as their close friends and siblings. Daniel, for example, at the age of 10, was strong in mathematics. His reading and writing skills fell within the average range. One Friday evening, Daniel was irritable and told his father, "I wish I was smart like Timothy. The teacher uses his essays as examples of good writing a lot, and he's on a higher reading level than me." His father tried to comfort him by saying, "We all have our areas of strength. You are okay in reading and writing, and you are amazing in your math." Daniel was not comforted at all. He believed he had to excel in all areas to feel successful. One day, Timothy said to Daniel, "I wish I could get the math like you. You are so smart!" Daniel laughed and said, "Me? You're the smart one." Finally, both agreed that they were both smart, just in different ways. Daniel finally understood his father's words of reassurance.

No human being is tops in all areas. In fact, some children who struggle in school (but remain confident) can still realize they are as bright as their classmates and able to learn skills for life. Without confidence, many people aren't as available to learn and focus on their abilities. Rather, they may be using much of their energy to try to manage their insecurities, avoid taking on challenging situations, and camouflage their self-doubts. Hopefully, you can help your child to identify her strengths and gain confidence from them, so she is not afraid to work toward new goals.

When talking to your children, it might be helpful to ask them to reflect on their abilities in the following areas:

- their ability to make friends,
- their ability to keep friends,
- their ability to like themselves,
- their performance in academic subjects,
- their skill in at least one area of athletics,
- their talent in the arts (music, dance, theater, drawing, painting),
- their ability to look at the glass as half full rather than half empty,
- their talent at using humor to make others smile and laugh, and
- their ability to set goals and work toward them.

All these areas are important for children to think about in order to find their personal niche. Some children, like Daniel, initially identify strengths but still lack confidence because they believe they should be outstanding in all areas. Some people start to gain confidence when they realize they have an area of particular talent. Talents can foster confidence, but there is more to it than that.

There are people who have all the abilities they need to be successful in their chosen endeavors (i.e., work, relationships, hobbies) and yet have a poor self-image. It can be helpful for you to spend time explaining to your child that how he feels about himself is the best indicator of confidence level. If a child, for example, would pick himself as his best friend, then he is likely a confident child who truly appreciates himself—personality, abilities, and even his "warts"! The exception is if your child picks himself as his best friend because he's uncomfortable making friends or negotiating and compromising with peers or he doesn't realize the benefit of having others in his life.

CONFIDENCE MAKES BECOMING INDEPENDENT EASIER

When children are confident, they are more willing to explore new experiences and challenges. Children and adults who lack confidence often have an internal dialogue that says, "Uh-oh, I've never done this. I don't think I can do this. I need someone to help me" before they even attempt to handle the situation on their own. Their self-doubts can lead to feelings of helplessness and anxiety.

The internal dialogue of the confident individual is sometimes mistakenly assumed to be "I can handle everything!" As you read earlier, it is an unusual person who handles everything independently. Emma's internal dialogue is reflective of a truly confident person:

> Let me try this new dance. I may not get it at first, but if I can laugh at myself, I'll have fun. I can ask my best friend for help practicing, but I am pretty sure I'll figure out the new steps before the school dance in two weeks!

Learning new information or having new experiences can be rewarding for the confident child and lead to feelings of pride. This child would know that effort, even without total success, can still feel good. Being independent can increase confidence, and having confidence can increase one's willingness to be independent. They are intricately connected.

CONFIDENCE INCREASES WITH EACH SUCCESS

As you read earlier in this chapter, there are some children who try to compete with older siblings, be the best at all sports, and the smartest in every class at school. Henry, for example, constantly competed against his older sister, Gabby, who was the star of her soccer team and an A student. Henry also wanted to be the president of his class and get the lead in the school play. Henry felt he was

37

determined and confident, and would, therefore, succeed in all that he tried.

How do you think Henry felt when he became vice president of his class, got an important but not lead role in the school play, and made the school but not the travel soccer team? Many children would be pleased to have attained these achievements. Henry, unfortunately, was not one of these children. He was left feeling frustrated and defeated.

When people set realistic, reachable goals, work for them, and attain them, their confidence generally increases. The following are some tips for helping your children to set realistic goals:

- Take time to discuss what they would like to achieve now and what their long-term goals are.
- Help them figure out what they can realistically do at this time and then set a goal for a step beyond this (such as moving up a ladder toward a larger goal).
- Remind your children that all people are different and there is no need to compete against a sibling or friend.
- Help them understand that there are many paths to success and they have to find their own talents (e.g., not all people are academic, athletic, artistic, and so forth).
- Guide them to set expectations in line with their particular abilities.
- Help them to be resilient and remain confident, even while working to overcome obstacles, accept disappointments, and reevaluate the goals they set.

Henry set his goals so high that even partial success made him feel like a failure. On the other hand, while setting goals below one's ability seems less stressful and easier, it can deprive your child of the coping strategies to face and overcome challenges. Learning to strive when it's reachable but not easy can lead to confidence and a sense of competence.

CONFIDENCE INCREASES WITH PERIODIC "FAILURE"

"If at first you don't succeed, try, try again" and "No sense banging your head against a brick wall" are two old sayings that are both wise, yet contradictory. Let's take a few moments to discuss these.

Does your child ever want to give up quickly after trying a new experience because success was not immediate? This may be okay, on occasion, if there was no necessity and little interest or motivation to learn a particular task. However, too often when children develop a habit of giving up prematurely, they also give up the chance to try, fail, learn from their failure, try a new path, fail some more, learn some more strategies, and eventually succeed. From this, they can learn that initial failure is not the end of the world. They become more confident knowing that even early difficulties or failures can mean that hard work and realistic expectations can still lead to eventual success.

Some children understand how to persevere. They work and work and work. They are proud of their efforts and feel like their work ethic pays off. Sometimes, however, this perseverance can be detrimental. When children or adults persist at trying one strategy to achieve their goals even though it didn't work the first few times, it can lead to a sense of frustration and loss of confidence. At some point, perseverance just becomes perseveration, which is like a hamster running on a wheel without getting anywhere.

Children can benefit from your guidance in helping them to find a new strategy that might lead to better results. This can be a valuable lesson on the importance of flexible thinking, the benefits of asking for help when "stuck," and the fact that not all persistence is advantageous. Trying the same strategy over and over can give people headaches because they have metaphorically been "banging their heads against a brick wall."

CONFIDENCE VERSUS BRAVADO

Children may brag about their abilities without having the talent to back it up or the social awareness of how the bragging is perceived by others. Some classmates may think the person bragging must be telling the truth, so they begin to feel intimidated. Others may just roll their eyes and get frustrated with the person. Even when a child who brags is accurate in stating that his skills are exceptional, the bragging can lead to alienation from peers.

Ramon came home from school one day and told his mother,

> Jason was so annoying. He was bragging about what a great baseball player he is and how he will one day play in the major leagues. He may be the best baseball player in our small town, but he's acting like he's the next Derek Jeter.

Jason's bravado bothered Ramon and several of his friends so much that they started to avoid hanging out with Jason.

As was the case with Jason, bravado can backfire. Rather than impressing others, it can lead other kids to avoid the company of the person bragging. This is especially true when one's ability does not live up to the boasting. Because boasting or bragging can be problematic, sometimes parents encourage their children to be modest about their talents or skills. The trouble with this is that there are times when it is not advantageous to be humble and highlight only the talents of others. Imagine going on a job interview and not trying to sell yourself. Bragging is the extreme, but having the confidence to describe why you are special is an important skill to learn in preparation for eventual job or college interviews. A great way to show your child how to find the balance between sharing and remaining quietly humble about his talents is to model how you handle this situation.

Many children could benefit from learning that "time, place, and person" are relevant when deciding whether to talk about their special qualities or to remain quietly humble. With the right people, at the right time, and in the right setting, it can be great for children to share their successes and achievements. Frequently, a good time to do this is when relatives or close family friends visit, and you know they would love to share in your children's happiness.

Children and adults brag for a number of different reasons, such as

- not wanting others to see that they are actually insecure,
- wanting to believe what they say to boost their confidence,
- wanting to impress others, and
- wanting to feel important while gaining popularity.

What can you do to help your child if you notice she is bragging? The following are some tips on teaching your child to have true confidence rather than bravado:

- Over dinner or during quiet car rides, try asking how kids react when someone says something in a bragging tone. This allows your child to think about it (focused on other kids) rather than potentially feeling criticized.
- Remind your child that actions speak louder than words ("It's better to let your friends experience your skills and success rather than repeatedly hear about it from you").
- If your child is trying to impress other kids to be liked, spend some time talking about what real friendships are all about.

- If you catch your child bragging, wait for a quiet time and avoid being critical, but ask about what she was thinking while bragging and what reaction she wanted (this can increase self-reflection).
- Encourage your child to talk to you about things she is proud of, and then discuss the pros and cons of sharing these perceptions with peers.

Sometimes, good friends, as well as relatives, want to hear and be able to share in your child's accomplishments and enjoy knowing about your child's talents. If it were a black-and-white situation and children never shared successes with peers, it would be easier for children to avoid bragging. However, because sharing strengths as well as weaknesses allows others to truly know your child, it is more a matter of when, how, and where to share this information and with whom.

HOW COMPLIMENTS CAN ACTUALLY DIMINISH A CHILD'S CONFIDENCE

Many times, when children succeed at tasks, others compliment them with phrases such as, "I knew you could win the spelling bee!" and "Can't wait to see what you can do in next week's lacrosse match. You were amazing today at practice!" These well-meaning comments can put unintentional stress on a child, who may then fear that success leads to higher and higher expectations and more and more pressure.

It is inevitable that expectations are going to be placed on each of us. When this happens to your child, and the new expectations are motivating for him, it can lead to his setting and reaching higher yet realistic goals. What can you do to protect your child from feeling undue pressure when people around him "raise the bar" for what they expect him to do in the future?

The following are some ways parents can help their children ward off unnecessary pressures as a result of being complimented:

- When a neighbor says to your child, "Wow, you made the honor roll. I bet you'll make the high honor roll next semester," remember that the neighbor is probably trying to be encouraging, but feel free to respond, "We are celebrating this accomplishment. As long as she tries, we are proud of her any day!"
- When your son comes home and tells you his best friend said he's the "alpha dog" in his grade, you know it means he is socially powerful and he feels always being looked up to places too much pressure on him. You might say, "Just be yourself. If they look up to you just because you are being you, that's great, but if they don't, they don't. We just want you to be happy and be proud of your choices!"
- At a party in your home, you overhear several of your daughter's friends comment on how she's "awesome" because she always "has the best new designer clothes and newest phone." Luckily, she speaks with you about her discomfort with these compliments, saying, "I hate the pressure of always having to have the best things. We're not made out of money." You might calm her down by saying, "Items are great if you enjoy them, but items don't define you. Remember who you are, and those who really are your true friends will admire you for that!"

When adults give concrete compliments (e.g., "It was impressive how you passed the ball and assisted in getting the goal!"), children can understand why the compliment was given. In addition, these comments can help children accept what led to the high praise, rather than think, "She always tells me I'm the best just because she's my mom."

Especially during the teenage years, adolescents may roll their eyes as they talk about well-meaning comments or actions on the part of their parents, relatives, or others. Kiesha, for instance, mentioned, "My mom keeps saying I'm the prettiest and smartest kid but I don't apply myself." Kiesha believed she wasn't the prettiest or the smartest. She said, "I wish my mom was just honest. Maybe she could have told me, especially when I was younger, that I'm pretty enough and smart enough, and I should be happy being me." Kiesha knew her parents were trying to encourage her, but her mother's message was lost because of the exaggerations.

To summarize, it is important to learn to identify when your child is feeling uncomfortable under the pressure of compliments. Sometimes, children don't even know why they are uncomfortable and may not be able to express their stress to you. Asking open-ended questions may help them reflect on how they felt after getting a compliment (e.g., "When Aunt Carrie said she can't wait to see you win the science fair competition again next year, how did that make you feel?"). In addition, giving specific and realistic compliments can give children and teenagers the message that you are *really* paying attention and there are reasons for the compliments other than just the fact that you love them.

PARENTAL PITFALLS WHILE TRYING TO INCREASE YOUR CHILD'S CONFIDENCE

There are several common pitfalls for parents as they try hard to raise a confident child. After you have an opportunity to think about these pitfalls, it can be easier to avoid them. Some of the pitfalls include sharing your anxieties, criticizing instead of critiquing, and trying to give your child what you missed in childhood.

Sharing Your Anxieties

Raising children and wanting to protect them can naturally create anxiety for parents. How can you keep them safe? How can you let them venture off on their own? How can you protect them from failures? How can you know whether their friends will lead them in a negative direction? There are more questions than a book could hold. These are not unrealistic or unnecessary questions. How you deal with your apprehension can make the difference between raising a confident child who is comfortable becoming independent and a child who fears and lacks confidence for handling common life experiences.

An example of how anxiety can significantly affect children might help to clarify this issue. From the ages of 2 to 12, Anna moved from foster home to foster home. She was exposed to violence and frequent transitions and was not given the opportunity to have a constant, loving family situation. Even though a wonderful family adopted her when she was 12, she was always fearful she would be alone once again. When she had children, Anna tried to keep them close, thinking this would give them the sense of security she never had and they would become confident individuals. Unfortunately, Anna's son did not know of his mother's past and intentions. Rather, he believed his mother did not have confidence in his ability to be independent, which was why she was always hovering. For instance, she welcomed his friends to their home and let them play in her son's room only if the door was left open so she could hear what going on and be nearby if needed. She never let her son go to a friend's house to play or to sleep over. Anna's daughter sensed her mother's anxiety and felt obligated to make her mother feel better, even at the cost of taking on challenges (e.g., she came home right after school each day rather than staying for sports or clubs). Anna's daughter did not allow herself the chance to engage in these social opportunities and activities and, therefore, deprived herself of the "growing" experience that breeds confidence that she can take on such new situations on her own.

Although the example of Anna may not describe the life you led, her apprehensions for the safety of her children may be feelings you can relate to. If you ever feel anxious about sending your children into the world, wondering if they will be safe and successful, you are not alone. There are many parents who cry after sending their smiling child to kindergarten on that first day of school, concerned that they are not going to be there to protect their young child from any and all dangers, real and imagined. Parents may also be concerned that the teacher will not anticipate all of their child's needs and that the child would therefore be neglected and unhappy. Most teachers are trained to help children navigate through their school day and support them when difficulties arise. It can also help both parents and children reduce feelings of anxiety if the children have some ability to be independent in an age-appropriate manner as well as to ask assertively for help if needed.

If your anxiety causes you to struggle with how to let your child grow and venture out to try new experiences, the following are some tips to help you:

- Think about whether your worries involve irreversible or extremely dangerous situations; if not, remind yourself of this.
- Think about balancing the worry of overprotection and the risk of depriving your child of the chance to gain confidence from being independent because of your instinct to protect.

- Parenting naturally includes some worries, but a child who picks up on parental anxiety can be too fearful to explore and can miss opportunities to gain confidence.

Criticizing Instead of Critiquing

Have you ever tried to calmly talk with your child, just to have him roll his eyes, act like he is deaf to your words, or walk away? There are some subtle ways you can try to decrease this "tuning out" reaction. Children, especially tweens and teens, are looking to make their own decisions and can easily feel disrespected and insulted when a parent disagrees. Therefore, they may react from their feelings rather than focus on the possibility that parents might truly have more insight or more experiences to guide them. One way to help children listen more and react less is to critique rather than criticize when you disagree with their decisions or actions. If you critique, it means you are talking with your child about why you disagree and the potential consequences you foresee. If you criticize, it means you are judging her abilities in general.

The following are examples of parents trying to give the same message, one critiquing and one criticizing:

The critiquing parent: "I understand why you think that way, but have you considered all the consequences that might happen if you follow that path? I really believe if you try it this way, you may find you'll be happier in the end."

The criticizing parent: "How can you be so ridiculous and immature and think that your plan is going to work out?"

It's helpful to think like a teenager before giving feedback to your child or teen. Remember, you were once that age! If you expect a teenager to get angry about what you are saying, take a moment and think about whether there is a more approachable way you can have the conversation.

There are some situations in which you will have to quickly disagree and put a stop to your child's actions rather than taking the time to ask her to evaluate her plan. Save your immediate and strong reactions for times when your child is truly at risk of being physically hurt or making a situation irreversibly worse. When Eli was 12 years old, for example, he was about to dive into the shallow end of the community swimming pool. With little time to spare, his mother ran over and yelled, "Stop! You're about to crack your head open! What were you thinking?" After initially catching his attention, Eli's mom lowered her voice and said, "Eli, I want you to think about what could have happened to you if you dove and hit your head on the bottom. If you want to dive, go to the deep end of the pool." Eli was about to get defensive but then realized his mother had saved him from accidentally hurting himself badly and he hadn't been thinking of consequences beforehand.

When your child is making less serious mistakes, the following are some strategies you can try:

- Compliments work—is there a part of your child's thinking that you respect, agree with, or even admire? If so, highlight it!
- Pick a time to have the discussion when you know that you and your child can both spend the time really talking and listening to each other.
- Explore potential positive and negative consequences of your child's plan.
- If your child gets angry, and you are tempted to say things such as, "Don't be rude or disrespectful," think about using the following substitute message: "I know you are angry at

me right now, but try to explain your anger in words so I can understand why you are so angry."

- Agree to have another discussion after you both have time to think about the current one (or have time to cool down).
- Remember that there are often crossroads with no one right path.
- Obviously, hitting doesn't enhance communication!

Trying to Give Your Child What You Missed in Childhood

When parents hold their newborn, they often think about all their hopes for this young child's future. Health and happiness are generally the first thoughts. After this, however, parents may think about their own childhoods, what they loved and what they missed out on.

Over time, if parents continue to focus on their own history, they may miss focusing on the unique wishes, personality, and skills of their children. These parents are generally well intentioned but may unintentionally put undue pressure on their children to please their parents by enjoying what the parents wish for them. Sometimes children end up sharing the same interests as their parents after being exposed to a variety of activities. However, when these children are asked to repeatedly engage in activities that made their parents feel happy as children even though the children do not like or excel in them, these children may feel inadequate and misunderstood. They may lose the confidence that comes from being heard and respected for their own wants and desired activities.

For example, Douglas, at the age of 11, found academic work to be relatively easy and gratifying. However, he struggled with most athletic and artistic pursuits. His father, who worked hard to become a doctor, regretted the fact that he never joined a team sport and missed having the experience of team camaraderie. He kept encouraging Douglas to join the soccer team or the baseball team. When Douglas calmly explained that he wasn't interested in either, his father became insistent. When Douglas said he wanted to try out for the debate and chess teams, his father was annoyed that his son would refuse to follow his suggestions, which came from his own experiences. His father, unfortunately, did not realize that Douglas could gain the team camaraderie experience in both endeavors in which he was interested. Douglas finally gave in to his father's wishes but spent most of the time sitting on the bench and silently resenting his father. Douglas lost confidence as he tried and failed to play well, and he felt his father did not believe in his ability to make independent decisions.

Clearly, each person is unique. What worked for parents when they were young or what they longed for as children may not be the right course of action for their children. Although Douglas could not enjoy or meet his father's expectations for him as an athlete, his sister shared a love of athletics with her father. Spend some time thinking about what you believe are your child's strengths, interests, and desires. This could make for an important conversation between you and your child. Your child may agree to try out an activity that you enjoyed. You may similarly want to learn more about the interests of your child. Parents can be pleasantly surprised to find that they enjoy the activity that was introduced to them by their child. You may find that you share more things in common than you realized!

WAYS YOU CAN INCREASE YOUR CHILD'S CONFIDENCE

You just read about some ways to avoid the pitfalls that might accidentally diminish the confidence of your child. There are many proactive ways to increase her confidence, some of which were discussed at the start of this chapter and some which are reviewed in the upcoming chapters, in which you will learn many ways to help your child feel competent and gradually become self-sufficient. At this point, let's focus on a few key ingredients for parenting an increasingly confident child.

Dealing With Your Child's Insecurity

It is a testament to the trusting, loving relationship you have with your child if she turns to you when feeling insecure. When your child puts on a brave face to the world and then cuddles up with you and cries about fears and trepidations, you have been given a gift. This gift is the openness of your child and your child's faith that you have the ability to guide and support her at her most vulnerable times.

The following are a few tips for helping your children when they feel insecure:

- Communicate confidence. While guiding and supporting your child, let her know whether you believe she can handle the situation with your advice or whether she should get help from others. There can be confidence in knowing when, and who, to ask for help (e.g., "I think you might want to talk to your math teacher about this problem, but here are some ideas that might help you for now").
- Remember that trying to convince your child that he can independently handle a challenge is only helpful if he can! Encouraging your child to attempt to handle a challenge that cannot be attained at that point may only breed a sense of further insecurity and lack of confidence. If this occurs, you should help him to set more attainable goals.
- Sometimes just listen. That may be all your child is looking for at that moment.

- If your child isn't ready to talk, remind him that you are there when he is ready.
- Share some relevant, appropriate insecurities you had as a child and how you overcame them. This is a great way to model coping strategies without a child becoming defensive. Sometimes you could even refer to historical figures who often failed but eventually succeeded (e.g., Ernest Hemingway's writing was repeatedly rejected by publishers until he finally was acknowledged for the quality of his work).

If despite your best efforts to help build up his confidence level, your child continues to feel insecure, it might be useful to seek professional advice. For instance, some children are so terrified of taking on new challenges and experiences that they convince themselves that they can't so that they avoid the anxiety that comes with the attempt.

Loving in a Way Your Child Understands

There has been a lot written about love. In Gary Chapman and Ross Campbell's book, *The 5 Love Languages of Children: The Secret To Loving Children Effectively*, they mentioned the following languages: gifts, quality time, words of affirmation, acts of service, and physical touch. Your infant feels your love through your physical touch, body language, and voice intonations. As your child gets older, spending time with her, giving positive comments and hugs, smiling when she enters a room, and giving her thoughtful (although not always materialistic) gifts can also communicate your love.

If your child hears you say "I love you" in a language he does not understand, your message will be lost. Take a few minutes to think about how your child knows you love him. Michael knew his dad loved him because of his expressions of joy and the amount of time his dad spent talking with him about his work and coaching his sports teams, despite being exhausted from long days at work. Alexa felt special and loved by her parents when they both listened to her social problems and never judged but always guided her when she tried to navigate through tough times.

Can you figure out how your child perceives your style of loving? If you're not sure, try the following strategies:

- When there is time, open the conversation and listen to the ways your child has felt closest to you and knows he is loved.
- Spend time doing things and talking with your child—watch when your child is the most relaxed, open, and responsive to you. That probably indicates you are creating a setting for closeness.
- When you are trying to be caring and close to your child and your child is disengaged, take some time to think about whether your timing is off or whether your loving "style" is not the right one for that child at that time.
- Of course, if your tween or teen pushes you away, it may be due to a problem, but more likely, it's just the age! During these years, periodic sharing of insecurities are special opportunities for you to help and acknowledge that your child feels loved and safe to confide in you despite the developmental desire for independence.

A child who knows she is loved is a child who tends to be more confident. Children show and perceive being loved differently at different developmental stages. For instance, an infant, toddler, and young child may crave the cuddling and hugs from parents, combined with smiles, soothing vocal tones, and loving words. When parents take the time to put their children to bed at night with hugs, smiles, and maybe even a bedtime story, it can help children feel safe to sleep and know they are loved. Older children may still want the hugs but may push parents away, at first when these hugs are given in public and later even in private moments. Parents who are flexible in how they show their love (e.g., giving compliments, being supportive, paying attention, showing interest in the child's activities, giving hugs, using loving words) can try to show their children this love in a way that can be accepted, even through the teenage years.

Offering Consistent, Day-to-Day Support

When growing up, fears about friendships and school can be overwhelming for some children at some times. Being socially excluded or being popular are both potentially stressful for children. Doing well in school and taking on more accelerated classes or struggling to understand the grade-level work can both be challenging as well.

If your child sees you as a sounding board, she can often feel more confident managing her day-to-day stresses. She knows she is not alone to figure out how to work through difficult times. When you are asked to listen to your child's thoughts and concerns, it may sometimes be hard not to judge. If she is being bullied by a friend, you may think, "Get rid of that friend. She doesn't treat you right." This may accidentally give your child the message that you don't have confidence that she can figure out a way to handle the social difficulty. On the other hand, if you try to have your child keep the friendship and resolve the conflict, despite being bullied, your child may feel misunderstood and unable to cope.

Academically, your child may come to you, and you may not always be sure when to encourage independent perseverance, when you should try to help with the homework, and when you should encourage your child to speak with the teacher. Before offering advice, it's helpful to

- hear your child's perspective,
- hear how your child would like to handle the situation,
- hear how your child would like you to respond to the discussion and/or the situation,
- ask your child about the potential consequences (good or bad) of that option, and
- ask whether he wants to hear of a situation you experienced that is somewhat similar (just make sure it's a useful story with a "lesson" included).

SUMMARY

In this chapter you read about what confidence means, why it is important to foster it in your children, and how you can help raise confident children while avoiding the pitfalls that can lead to diminished confidence. Truly confident children can take healthy risks, laugh with themselves when they make mistakes, and seek out support when needed. In the next chapter, you will learn about how to help your child to manage small as well as larger tasks and responsibilities.

CHAPTER 3

EXECUTIVE FUNCTIONING SKILLS: TEACHING YOUR CHILD TO MANAGE TASKS LARGE AND SMALL

Successful adults are generally those who have strong executive functioning skills. These same skills are often helpful for students as they strive for success. Whether a person is working, studying, or taking care of a family, the abilities you will read about in this chapter are key to being effective. You will read about how to help your child develop these important skills, for now and for the long term.

What do professionals mean when they refer to *executive functioning skills*? There are many definitions and many skills that fall under this label. In this chapter, we focus on some of the necessary ingredients for current and future independence, including

- learning to identify short-term as well as long-term goals;
- learning to figure out whether your goals are realistic;
- learning to organize how you will reach your goals;
- organizing the materials you need for the tasks;
- initiating, or starting to work;
- prioritizing what to work on and in what order;
- maintaining self-motivation;
- persevering, not perseverating;
- thinking flexibly to switch strategies when needed; and
- acquiring skills specific to learning.

In reviewing this list, you will be able to see how you use many of these skills daily or even many times each day. Think about how useful, or even necessary, these abilities are for your child as well. Before continuing to read, take a minute to reflect on how you encourage the executive functioning skills in your child and how you stress their importance.

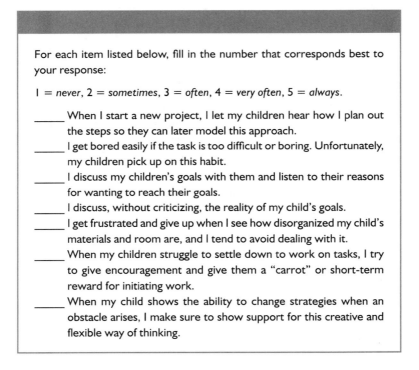

For each item listed below, fill in the number that corresponds best to your response:

1 = *never*, 2 = *sometimes*, 3 = *often*, 4 = *very often*, 5 = *always*.

_____ When I start a new project, I let my children hear how I plan out the steps so they can later model this approach.

_____ I get bored easily if the task is too difficult or boring. Unfortunately, my children pick up on this habit.

_____ I discuss my children's goals with them and listen to their reasons for wanting to reach their goals.

_____ I discuss, without criticizing, the reality of my child's goals.

_____ I get frustrated and give up when I see how disorganized my child's materials and room are, and I tend to avoid dealing with it.

_____ When my children struggle to settle down to work on tasks, I try to give encouragement and give them a "carrot" or short-term reward for initiating work.

_____ When my child shows the ability to change strategies when an obstacle arises, I make sure to show support for this creative and flexible way of thinking.

Raising a child with strong executive functioning skills isn't always easy, but recognizing that your child has these skills can allow you to feel more comfortable knowing he is getting prepared for independent life. Learning these skills does not have to be an arduous task. For instance, when Kenny was planning his party for his 10th birthday, he loved creating the invitation list, writing down what foods would be served, making a grocery list and then shopping with his mother, and so forth. The organization and follow-through that was necessary for his party can help him as he goes through school and has to be organized and persevere at reaching other goals. Many times, children can have fun developing these planning skills as they set up parties or art projects or create new rules for games. Even though Kenny was using executive functioning skills, he didn't realize he was—he just went ahead and planned his party.

While developing executive functioning skills can seem like fun, and your child may not even realize these skills are being strengthened, there may be other times when learning executive functioning skills doesn't always feel natural or comfortable for children. For instance, how many children are excited about setting time aside to prioritize studying spelling words rather than spending all their time playing? How many adults also prefer to play rather than initiate, organize, persevere at, and finish tasks that are not particular areas of interest (or are just plain boring) but are necessary for them, their work, or their family? Luckily, for both children and adults, the gratification they feel from success and reaching goals can compensate for the short-term discomfort.

LIFE WITHOUT STRONG EXECUTIVE FUNCTIONING SKILLS

Some people are born with a trust fund and never have to work a day in their life. Even for these rare individuals, executive functioning skills play a role in giving them a sense of purpose and reaching gratifying goals.

Maggie, age 8, was a gregarious youngster who loved to live in the moment. She was spontaneous and upbeat. Her parents enjoyed her enthusiasm for life. When she had work to complete or tasks to focus on, her parents usually sat with her and told her what to do first, second, and third until she finished her work. Once one task was completed, they presented her with the next one. Maggie did accomplish her schoolwork but did not do her homework independently. Over the next few years, Maggie's self-confidence began to wane as her friends spent more time planning out what they wanted to do and strived to reach their goals. Unfortunately, Maggie had never developed the early skills for planning and working independently toward attaining her goals.

In sixth grade, Maggie, now 11, and her classmates had to each do a music project in which they picked a musician, reviewed that person's history and music, presented pictures, and put the project on a poster board or made a Prezi presentation. The students were given 4 weeks to complete the project. One week before it was due, most of Maggie's classmates had already picked the project, initiated the plan, prioritized their steps, and persevered at moving toward their goal of having a finished project. Maggie was still casually trying to think about which musician she wanted to highlight for her project.

Imagine how Maggie felt when the project deadline arrived. Her best friend walked into class with a large poster board. Another friend was excited to share her Prezi presentation and show how she incorporated pictures, words, and even a YouTube video into it. Maggie tried to convince her mom that she was ill that day rather than go to school without a project. She didn't want to face the disapproval of her teacher and feel embarrassed in front of her friends. She was angry with her parents for not doing the project for her, and she told her mother she felt unable even to start this assignment.

There are many children like Maggie. They have good intentions without good follow-through. Parents have tried yelling at or lecturing them to focus and do their work. Others have taken away privileges, social time, or technology. These techniques may lead to short-term success because children do the work to avoid having an angry or disappointed parent and to avoid possible punishment. However, children may not learn the skills needed to complete work more easily, and they may not focus on the fact that doing work can lead to them feeling proud of having mastered the task and feeling pleased with themselves. Instead, they may just feel the adrenalin rush that comes with a fear of having negative consequences as the motivator for getting work done.

Even with a desire to please, children without strong executive functioning skills may not always respond to or benefit from parental pressures because they have to develop the basic abilities to start, work on, and finish tasks. They may also feel that their parents are not supportive, despite the fact that the parents are expending much energy trying to convince them to work, because the child may feel unable even to start the work without one-on-one guidance from a grown-up. If this situation sounds familiar, you know how exhausting it is to remind your child to get started and organize his work while he seems to care much less than you do about his responsibilities.

The truth is that without the skills, many children seem to avoid and not care about tasks, but they actually have a sense of inadequacy and puzzlement about how to plan, start, and complete the tasks. This sense of inadequacy makes some children avoid tasks and feel inferior to their peers who have stronger executive functioning skills. When children don't have these skills, they may truly flounder later on when starting a job or going to college when the expectation is that they can independently follow through on what is expected. For that reason, we focus most of this chapter on goal setting and task management, even though executive functioning is an umbrella term that includes many other skills as well.

IDENTIFYING SHORT-TERM AND LONG-TERM GOALS

Every day, children, as well as adults, automatically take care of many tasks because of goals they want to reach. As an adult, you pay bills to avoid having your electricity turned off, you pick up your children from play dates so that they are home for dinner, and you clean dishes so that you have clean plates. Children put shoes on before leaving for school so they are not barefoot, teased, or cold in the wintertime. They do their homework, and hopefully remember to place the completed work in their backpacks, so that they meet the academic expectations that were set for them.

Children with executive functioning skills may seamlessly work to reach their daily goals. Without executive functioning abilities, children may forget what homework to do, leave whatever work was completed at home, and may not even focus on eating breakfast until their stomach growls once they are in school.

Because short-term goals are often the first steps in reaching long-term goals, it may be helpful to talk about setting long-term goals first. For instance, Jayden, age 10, is already talking about wanting to go to a good college. This is a realistic goal for him if he is willing to strive to attain the short-term goals that will enable him to reach this long-term goal. The following are some tips for helping your child identify short-term goals (immediate or those attainable within a short period):

- Ask your child about his dreams for the future (in the next section you will learn ways to help your child to determine whether the dreams are realistic).
- Listen to why your child has specific dreams, because these reasons can serve as motivation later on when perseverance becomes necessary.
- Have a conversation about what can be done today to start making the long-term goal possible (e.g., practicing a backflip

to improve a gymnastics routine to do well eventually at a national competition).

- If your child is not cooperative about completing the necessary steps toward reaching the goal, remind her that it is her goal and her eventual disappointment if she fails to reach it.
- Children often learn by example. Think about the steps you took to reach your goals and then discuss them with your child.

If you visualize a ladder with many steps to get to the top, you can think of each step as a short-term goal and the top of the ladder as the long-term goal. Sometimes it can even be helpful to draw a picture of a ladder and have your child write on each step the immediate and short-term goals with the ultimate goal on the top. He can color in each step that has been completed so it is easy to see the progress toward the top.

A short-term goal can be something quickly attainable (sometimes people refer to this as an *immediate goal*), or it can be a goal that is simply closer in time than a long-term goal. This can be confusing, so let's look at two examples. Max, age 15, wanted to make the high school baseball team. That was his long-term goal. Practicing hitting and pitching each day with his friends and parents and getting a certain percentage of hits when he was at bat and strikeouts against those trying to hit his pitches was his short-term goal. He attained this short-term goal within a month and reached his long-term goal soon after.

Benjamin wanted to become a doctor. However, the long-term goal at the top of his current ladder was to get an A on his chemistry midterm. His short-term goal, therefore, was to review all his notes and the chapter summaries 1 week before the exam and get a grade of at least 90 on the review tests in his chemistry book. Benjamin attained his short-term goal, although he had a bit more difficulty reaching his long-term goal. He learned that he had to reread each chapter in the future and not assume the summaries covered all the information.

Long-term goals are not written in stone. A toddler who wants to become a mermaid will hopefully have the flexible thinking to seek a more realistic goal over time! Max originally thought he would become a professional baseball player. Despite his success reaching his high school goals, he was later exposed to the world of finance and ended up majoring in business in college. A child who is open to new information is a child who can change ultimate goals on the basis of that new knowledge. As your child thinks about goals, remember that a goal is a dream you work toward.

IDENTIFYING REALISTIC VERSUS UNREALISTIC GOALS

Young children often have a rich fantasy life, dreaming of becoming superheroes, mermaids, baseball stars, and other such difficult to attain or even impossible ambitions. Unrealistic goals are common to small children. Even older children have these dreams but gradually turn unrealistic goals into more realistic alternatives. When your children confidently share an unrealistic goal with you, it can be helpful to

- accept their creative thinking,
- acknowledge their desire to reach the particular goal,
- learn why they decided on that goal,
- allow very young children to express the goal as long as they do so safely (e.g., no flying out a window to act like Superman), and
- calmly discuss older children's goals without criticizing or demeaning them because elements of their unrealistic desires can be met in more realistic ways.

As children develop executive functioning skills, helping them differentiate between realistic and unrealistic expectations becomes increasingly important. For instance, Marsha was in seventh grade and wanted to get at least a B in science. That was her goal. She decided to start studying for the science final the day before the test. If Marsha had been able to differentiate realistic from unrealistic goals earlier, she would have been able to realize that this plan was not realistic for her because she had struggled throughout the year in this class. What would have been realistic for Abby, who found science class to be extremely easy, was not realistic for Marsha. Therefore, there is often no definitive realistic or unrealistic goal but rather an individualized attainable or unattainable goal at the time.

DETERMINING STEPS TOWARD REALISTIC GOALS

Going back to the example of the ladder, it can be helpful to spend time talking with your child about what he wants to achieve at the top and what steps he thinks will get him there. It is not always natural for a child to have this kind of mental organization of the steps toward the goals. The following are some suggestions to facilitate this:

- Give examples from your life, when you were a child, of the steps you took toward your goals and what you wanted at the top of your ladder.
- Some children shrug their shoulders when parents attempt to guide them in organizing their goals. They might prefer you to provide the answers and fix the situation for them; you can ask guiding questions, but allow your child to be actively involved in the brainstorming.

- The following guiding questions can help your child think about goals, although the language will have to be adjusted depending on the age of your child:

  (a) If you had a magic wand, what would you change in your life?

  (b) Can you work to have one of these changes happen?

  (c) Is your goal realistic or simply a wish that is fun to think about though you know it is impossible?

  (d) What would you like to do soon?

  (e) If you get what you want, would it keep you from reaching your goals for your future? For instance, if you miss a bunch of soccer practices to hang out with friends, will you still get to play in the games?

  (f) Would working hard toward your goal give you happiness or satisfaction?

  (g) What steps do you have to take now to work toward your long-term goal?

Many children set goals such as, "If I had a magic wand, I wouldn't go to school, and I could be with my friends all day." It takes some calm perseverance on the part of parents to use this short-term goal to build the critical thinking necessary for more serious choices. The following is how 10-year-old Robert's mother handled his response to her guiding questions:

Mother: Sounds like fun, but once you grow up you may wish you had more schooling so you could get the job you want. Didn't you mention that you want to be an architect?

Robert: Yeah, but I really just want to hang out with my friends and have fun all day! I'll worry about being an architect later.

Mother: Imagine you hang out all day and then don't get good test grades because you missed the lessons. Would you mind growing up to have a nice cardboard box and street corner to call home? I thought you wanted a house, computers, cars, and other things that you need money to buy.

Robert: Yeah, I guess you're right. I hate when you are so logical, Mom.

Mother: If you want to be an architect, what can you do now to start toward that goal? [*This would be the short-term goal.*]

Robert: Stay in school. Yes, I said it. Ugh!

Mother: Anything else?

Robert: Like what?

Mother: Maybe you can earn money now to pay for one of those large LEGO sets to build some new type of buildings! Building LEGO structures can help you have fun now and work toward your future dream as well.

Robert and his mom then spent time talking about how Robert could work toward his short-term goal of earning money for the large LEGO set. He then identified some steps needed to begin working toward his long-term goal of being an architect. He didn't spend a lot of time on this long-term goal, but it helped motivate him to stay in school, focus on his math, art, and other subjects he will need in the future.

Kids do not have to sacrifice everything enjoyable now for something that can occur 10 years in the future. However, you can help them see how some choices would prevent them from reaching their goals. In addition, sometimes thinking about a long-term dream can help kids realize they can do something fun today that is similar to what they want in the future.

READY, SET, GO

Once your child has determined a short-term goal, it's time to begin working toward it. A daily short-term goal (sometimes referred to as an *immediate goal* if it can be reached quickly) could be to finish homework so that your child has the rest of the evening to do other things. Many children struggle with getting started on homework. Initiation of any task can be a bit of a challenge for some children.

Your children may feel it's important to wait until a sudden motivation guides them to the table to begin work. Because this only happens infrequently for some children, it is wise to help them to break down the "getting started" steps into more manageable and less stressful segments because you will not always be there to be their cheerleader or drill sergeant!

The following are some steps to help your child:

1. Together with your child, figure out when the best time for homework is for her—as soon as she arrives home, after a quick snack, or even after dinner.
2. Experiment with how long she can study before needing a break, then schedule in breaks so each segment isn't over-whelmingly long.
3. Use the clock to set up the start and stop times for doing homework.
4. Figure out what materials are needed, and have your child put them on the table so she doesn't need to run and get a pencil, then run and get a notebook from the backpack, and so forth.

After following these steps, step back and see whether your child work independently or whether more guidance is needed.

If more guidance is needed, the next few sections of this chapter highlight skills your child should develop.

PRIORITIZING AND TIME MANAGEMENT

Some children who have a science project to complete just keep thinking of all the components of it but can't get started. They might be overwhelmed and not sure how to begin, even as the due date approaches. There can be a sense of anxiety and "impending doom" that overtakes children when they realize they are not going to be able to complete their project or be prepared for a big test in time. This is often the experience that children have when they are faced with a major task but have not learned how to manage their time and prioritize the steps necessary to meet the challenge.

Prioritizing, a key element in getting organized, can be made into a game. Before your child starts a task, let her explain all that is needed (without worrying about doing any of the steps at first). You can write down each step on separate index cards. After writing out all the cards, you and your child will see how many steps are needed. Then, organize the cards into what to do first, second, and so on. Seeing the one small assignment on Card 1 is relatively simple and less stressful for your child to undertake. Some kids enjoy making paper airplanes out of the index cards after they complete the task on it. Other kids make a checklist rather than use index cards, and they check off each step toward their goal—this allows them to track their progress visually. You can sometimes have fun learning these organizational and prioritizing skills!

Even young children can begin to learn time-management skills. The following are a few tips:

- Avoid scheduling every task and activity for your child. Otherwise, he may just follow your lead without focusing on how you scheduled the time for each activity.

- Give your child free time to plan what to do in a given amount of time (e.g., "What are you going to do now that you have an hour before dinner?").
- If your child plans a time-consuming activity when there is only a short time available before the school bus arrives, use this as a "teachable moment."
- During a teachable moment ask, "Do you think you might run out of time to finish this now? Do you mind leaving it and finishing it later, or should you wait to start it when you can finish it all at once?"
- Start showing them how to fill in a daily schedule, listing their activities, homework time, dinner time, play time, school time, and even bedtime.
- Give older children a blank daily schedule with hours listed. Have them plot the different activities for the day, and over time, they will learn whether their time estimates are realistic.

Time management can be more difficult for some children who tend to focus only on the present moment, feel anxious about planning and working toward larger goals, or struggle with impulsivity or difficulties focusing on details. The latter situation was true for 9-year-old Alex. Alex was diagnosed with attention-deficit/hyperactivity disorder at the age of 7 and took medication during the day. At night, when it was time to do his homework, the medication had often worn off, and his impulsivity, low frustration tolerance, and distractibility affected his ability to start his work and see it through to completion. Alex's mother often set up his nightly schedule, and Alex gave his input but was not able to design his own schedule. He needed frequent breaks and refocusing. Having fun when he completed small segments of his work was key to motivating him. He loved basketball, so his mother wrote each small segment of his homework on a separate page, and after Alex finished that segment, he crumpled up the paper and tried to toss it in the wastepaper basket from a distance. Alex did his work in an attempt to get more shots to land the paper in the basket. He kept trying to break his old record of getting the paper in the basket. His homework became more of a game than a stress.

If you feel that every evening is focused on trying to help your child complete homework, you may want to look at what supports are available in your local area. For instance, sometimes after-school homework clubs or homework support at a local YMCA can allow your child to finish the work before coming home and facing the distractions of the many fun activities at home. This is especially helpful for parents who work long hours or single parents who benefit from having another adult supporting homework completion.

HELPING YOUR CHILD SELF-MOTIVATE

Imagine how your daily routine would be different if your children were able to start, continue, and conclude all chores and tasks, as well as work toward goals without reminders to keep working and without you being their main inspiration to continue. Imagine how much less anxiety you will feel when your children eventually go off to college or move out and start a job, and you know that they are able to motivate themselves to initiate, prioritize, and complete responsibilities. Many parents would have a lot more time. Interested?

Of course, the main reason for helping children learn the skill of self-motivation is so that they can continue motivating themselves as they grow up and leave home. According to Isaac Newton, the famous physicist, an object at rest tends to remain at rest, and an object in motion tends to remain in motion. This theory can also apply to people. A child glued to the TV or computer often stays there for long periods. There is nothing wrong with this, at times, but let's discuss how to help your child get up and be productive.

Young children are often enthusiastic about taking on new tasks and new experiences, such as crawling, walking, speaking, and learning. Embracing this self-motivation to achieve later goals can make a huge difference in your child's willingness to try new things. Parenting by supporting your child's explorations is not always simple.

Chloe was a 3-year-old preschool student. During the summer, she went to day camp, where swimming was her favorite activity. One day, Chloe did not want the counselor to put her shoes on for her after swimming. Chloe managed to put them on herself and proudly showed this feat to the other children and her counselors. The head counselor had a difficult decision to make. She wanted to support Chloe's pride in her effort to be self-sufficient, but she also wanted to point out to Chloe that the shoes were on the wrong feet. If you were the counselor, what would you have done?

Chloe's counselor decided to let Chloe enjoy her accomplishment and let her go home with her shoes reversed. The counselor planned to present a game to the campers the following day about how they could figure out which shoe goes on which foot. In the meantime, Chloe's mother, noticing her daughter came home with her shoes on the wrong feet, called the counselor immediately and expressed anger at the counselor's "neglect." However, after hearing the counselor's rationale, the mother paused then said, "Thank you! I forgot to focus on the achievement and, rather, focused on the mistake."

Self-motivation increases when a child feels safe to try, even when the effort does not lead to immediate perfection, victory, or even progress. The following are some tips for fostering self-motivation:

- Praise for the effort, not only for the outcome.
- Ask your child how he feels about taking on a task, and reflect back the positive feelings (so he knows he's doing things to please himself, not just you).

- Don't jump in to help too fast if you believe your child can self-start, but remind her how she felt after starting past tasks.
- Kids watch parents. If you are self-motivated, feel free to explain your strategies for getting started and what motivates you to continue.
- By complaining about your own tasks, you may accidentally be teaching your child that having to start a task is stressful and annoying.

You may have heard about behavior modification plans to motivate children. This can be a useful way to encourage kids to work for the carrot or short-term reward and simultaneously start and work on their responsibilities. Adults often have behavior modification plans too, even when they don't realize it. How many salespeople work extra hard to get an end-of-the-year bonus? The bonus is their carrot!

If you decide to create a behavior modification plan with your child, be specific about what you are targeting, make sure you are targeting realistically attainable goals, and be specific about what the "reward" would be. Nonmaterialistic rewards (e.g., breakfast out with a favorite grandparent) can often be as rewarding as materialistic ones, so don't overlook them. However, if you reward every effort your child makes, he will learn to work for the carrot rather than for the sense of accomplishment. It's a balancing act. If a reward teaches a child the pride that comes with self-reliance and self-motivation, it is a great tool. If the reward becomes the goal itself, it may seem more like a bribe and should be rethought.

PERSEVERING BUT NOT PERSEVERATING

If your children can self-motivate and also initiate and prioritize tasks, the next step is to persevere, monitor progress, and keep their eye on the goal. Breaking larger tasks up into smaller sections allows children to get organized and not feel overwhelmed. To persevere, children may also benefit from breaking larger tasks into small sections they can complete in a single time-period.

Perseverance rarely happens at bedtime when a child is exhausted, has difficulty focusing, and can easily get frustrated. Pick a time when your child can focus, and ask him how he felt about himself after sticking to what he started. This simple question encourages self-monitoring: "How do you feel knowing you worked so hard and finished what you hoped to accomplish today?"

The tricky part about perseverance is that you don't want your child to get hyperfocused or stuck on one thought or approach that turns into perseveration, which we touched on in Chapter 2. *Perseveration* means doing the same thing over and over even when it doesn't lead to the desired goal.

Sarah and Rebecca, both age 11, were motivated to do well in school. When their teacher gave them a social studies research project to complete, they both got started quickly even though the due date wasn't for another 3 weeks. Sarah went home and made an outline of what her project would entail. She then used this information, along with her time-management skills, to break down the tasks into smaller, reachable segments. She worked on each small segment and asked for help when needed. Sarah completed the project 5 days before it was due and then reviewed it and practiced presenting it to family members. She felt comfortable handing in her work when the due date arrived. Sarah had persevered (worked efficiently to reach her goal).

Rebecca also worked hard on her project. She was planning on presenting information about the history and culture of the Navajo people. Rebecca was excited about her plan to make a blanket with the same materials that early Navajo tribe members had used. She spent many hours trying to get the right materials and learn how to create the blanket. Unfortunately, her exclusive focus on getting the materials before doing further research did not allow her to complete any part of her project by the due date. Rebecca had devoted as much time as Sarah did to the project, but she was not productive. She focused on a goal that was never reached. She did not consult others to see whether there was a strategy to reach this goal other than the one she had, which was to keep checking for her materials on Amazon, eBay, and other websites. She never explored whether the materials were even available anywhere at the time she was trying to do her project. Rebecca was perseverating (repeatedly focusing without moving forward) rather than persevering (repeatedly focusing and steadily moving forward).

Sarah's case demonstrates how sticking with a task can be beneficial. This focus on one activity is sometimes referred to as being compulsive. Sarah working on her project, the surgeon always checking that every instrument is accounted for before closing up a surgical patient, and the pilot double checking his engine and instruments are all examples of people showing healthy compulsive behaviors.

Lately, people have been talking a lot about OCD (obsessive–compulsive disorder), a disorder that leads a person to have unproductive, repetitive thoughts and/or behaviors. An example of this is the surgeon who scrubs so long his hands are raw and he never gets to start the surgery on time. It might be helpful to encourage being OC (O for obsessive and C for compulsive—a label made up for the sake of making a point!) rather than OCD. OC, unlike OCD, has many advantages, such as being efficient, being organized, thinking things through carefully, and thinking about a positive, realistic goal. In other words, if a person (child or adult) spends time thinking carefully about tasks and is organized in how to master goals, it becomes an advantage rather than a disadvantage and a psychiatric diagnosis. In many societies, without a certain degree of obsessive–compulsive traits, a person may struggle to function at a high level.

WHY FLEXIBLE THINKING IS IMPORTANT

Have you ever tried to do something only to run into a major obstacle, forcing you to change your strategy? Being able to adjust your plan is an example of *flexible thinking*. Flexible thinking allows us to avoid the frustration of realizing our approach to a task wasn't working and then putting in more effort using the same approach to achieve the same outcome. Becoming flexible thinkers can allow children to restructure their nightly routine if a guest comes over and their study time has to be changed, for example. Being a flexible thinker means that sometimes short-term goals have to be reevaluated and changed. Being a flexible thinker also means that a child (or adult) can change opinions as new information is gathered.

To help your child to develop these flexible thinking skills, here are some tips:

- Over dinner, try creating a game of "What Would You Do?" In this game, create a situation similar to what people do in the locked room game that is gaining popularity. The situation could be something your child may realistically encounter, or it may be a more general scenario. Throw in some roadblocks to see how you and your child could rethink the situation and come up with a new way to deal with it.
- Describe realistic and age-appropriate situations from your life when you had to use flexible thinking and rethink your plan. By doing this, you are modeling flexible thinking.
- In everyday life, a plan sometimes has to be changed or an attempt to solve a homework problem doesn't work. This is an authentic opportunity to discuss alternative approaches or responses.

HOW CURIOSITY FEEDS MOTIVATION

As you've seen so far in this chapter, part of executive functioning is the ability to say to yourself, "Okay, I'm starting a task I do not like, but I'm going to prioritize, set goals, and persevere until the task is done!" We also suggest that fostering curiosity is another way you can support your child to become motivated to start and then follow through on tasks. After all, a curious learner seeks out knowledge rather than just accepting it passively.

Children are never too young to discover the fun of learning and the power of knowledge. If they are always presented with facts and simply asked to memorize them, there is a risk of your children becoming passive learners. However, encouraging curiosity and inquisitiveness may lead them to seek more knowledge on their own. If your children seek extra knowledge, it may seem unrelated to what they should be doing, and they may have to refocus on the task at hand. The extra information learned, though, may be useful later on so it's important to consider whether the off-task exploration is worthwhile as a tangent at the moment.

Teachers and parents often seek a balance between presenting facts and helping children to brainstorm ideas and learn ways to pursue answers and information. When parents spend time with their children researching questions that their children raise, it not only helps children to develop research skills but also reinforces that the parents value the curious question and are willing to devote time to explore the answers with their children.

There are times when parents don't have to foster curiosity but simply appreciate it when it naturally occurs. Jeremy, for example, at the age of 18 months, often giggled and clapped his hands when he learned how to do a new, independent task, such as climbing some steps or opening the kitchen cabinet. This is a time to smile and enjoy the moments. Of course, this assumes your home is baby-proofed so that your child's curiosity doesn't lead to touching an open electrical outlet, finding chemicals in the kitchen cabinet, or discovering pills that could end up being ingested.

Although your typically developing 10-year-old, compared with the toddler, probably won't visibly show the same joy from new accomplishments, the same excitement may be present. If not, you can recreate that joy of learning by encouraging curiosity to think, know, and try new things. Remember that learning occurs whenever your child is awake, not just during school time. When your child overhears you expressing curiosity and excitement over thoughts, you also model the importance of "thinking outside the box" with your creative ideas and that it's okay to express excitement over ideas at any age.

LEARNING STYLES AND EXECUTIVE FUNCTIONING

There has been a lot of research and discussion about learning styles. Some researchers have concluded that learning style discussions are not applicable to education, and others have suggested that learning styles do, in fact, have a place in education. We believe it's helpful to identify your child's learning styles and talk about this with your child. People who are aware of their learning styles can use this information to play to their strengths. Like curious learners, self-aware learners develop their executive functioning skills by taking charge of their learning.

Think about whether you have a preferred learning style, whether it's visual, auditory, kinesthetic (hands-on), and so forth. When you study material, take on responsibilities, and organize your life, do you rely more on one sensory modality (e.g., auditory, visual) than others? Your children may also have a preferred or more comfortable style of learning that fits them as individuals.

Some children, for example, learn best when there is a social component (e.g., group work), others learn through imitation, and many learn through a combination of their senses. Charles's teacher felt he was daydreaming a lot in class because he looked at his desk rather than at her during lessons. His teacher benefitted from learning that he was distracted by visual input when he was listening, and he was a strong auditory learner. In fact, Charles was attentive during lessons and looked away to focus more fully on his auditory input. Tricia, however, learned far more easily when she was touching materials (e.g., math manipulatives, science materials) because she was a kinesthetic learner. There is no "right" learning style.

Learning styles and focusing preferences can differ from one child to another, even in the same family. In school, there are even a variety of different chairs in some classrooms that suit each child. A stand-up desk with a bar that can be quietly moved by a student's leg or a wobbly chair that acts like a Pilates ball on which a child has to maintain his center of gravity are sometimes options for students who like to move a bit while listening. For other students, a regular "formal" classroom chair and other seating opportunities are now sometimes available and attract kids who often benefit from the chance to pick from a choice of seating arrangements.

Take some time to figure out how your child learns best—even by asking your child how she learns most easily—and then discuss this with her teachers. When your younger child brings home an assignment she's struggling with, offer to adapt it to her learning preferences. Ask an older child who complains about not understanding or not being able to focus on an assignment, "What do you think would make this information more 'digestible' for you?" Then help him find a way to use his preferred sensory channels. If you take the extra time to show your child how to direct her sensory focus and take charge of her learning early on, she will be prepared to advocate for herself later in life and create learning supports that take advantage of her unique strengths.

SUMMARY

In this chapter, you learned about some key executive functioning skills so that you can help your child develop them. Being competent in these areas is not just valuable for school but also important in life. In the next two chapters, you will read about how strong decision-making and frustration-tolerance abilities can also lead children to become more independent as they get older and leave home.

CHAPTER 4

DECISION MAKING: TIPS FOR HELPING YOUR CHILD MAKE HEALTHY CHOICES

When children have decision-making and problem-solving skills, they are on the road toward successful independence. To develop these abilities, children benefit from learning how to evaluate all their options to make the best choice in a particular situation. Once they learn to do this, they are better able to use their critical thinking skills. In addition, learning ways to compromise and negotiate as well as how to handle interpersonal, academic, and daily challenges can increase a child's confidence.

Parents, as you know, play a major role in helping their children to develop problem-solving skills. In this chapter, you will learn some key ways to recognize the "teachable moments" when modeling or teaching decision-making skills comes naturally. Children provide us with many of these moments as they go from stage to stage in their development. You may frequently hear your child (toddler through adolescent) say, "NO! I want to do it my way!" At this time, if your child's way of handling things does not put him in immediate danger, you can seize the opportunity to step away from the potential power struggle, while still presenting options and possible positive and/or negative consequences of the selected choice.

Before reading further in this chapter, take a minute to reflect on how you foster the development of decision-making and problem-solving skills in your child.

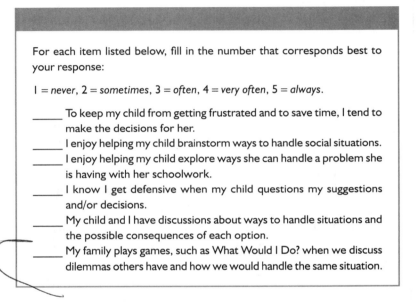

For each item listed below, fill in the number that corresponds best to your response:

1 = *never*, 2 = *sometimes*, 3 = *often*, 4 = *very often*, 5 = *always*.

_____ To keep my child from getting frustrated and to save time, I tend to make the decisions for her.

_____ I enjoy helping my child brainstorm ways to handle social situations.

_____ I enjoy helping my child explore ways she can handle a problem she is having with her schoolwork.

_____ I know I get defensive when my child questions my suggestions and/or decisions.

_____ My child and I have discussions about ways to handle situations and the possible consequences of each option.

_____ My family plays games, such as What Would I Do? when we discuss dilemmas others have and how we would handle the same situation.

DECISION MAKING AND PROBLEM SOLVING AS YOUR CHILD GROWS

As children get older, they are more capable of weighing options and thinking about more than yes or no decisions, and they are better able to anticipate the consequence of each possible choice. Your child's age, personality, maturity level, self-reflection skills, coping strategies, and ability to think through choices can all affect what parenting style works best to teach independent decision making. Whoever said parenting was easy when you have so much to consider? Hang in there!

Of course, it's normal to have children progress through developmental stages at a slightly different pace from siblings or friends without this indicating any reason for concern. However, as you read the following sections, know that they are general guidelines and you have to determine which strategies fit your particular child best.

Are the Terrible Twos Really Terrible?

In Chapter 1, we mentioned "the terrible twos." This sometimes challenging stage is a prime opportunity to start teaching your child how to make decisions. Toddlers face decisions daily, such as whether to use the toilet or the diaper, whether to demand the bottle when given a cup, and when physically capable of walking, whether to walk or continue to crawl.

You may enjoy watching your toddler explore, but parents are often on "high alert" when the curious toddler tries to explore an electrical socket or tries to figure out how to open the screen door to run outside to play. One of the many benefits of childproofing your home (e.g., using electric outlet covers; locking cabinet and outside doors; making sure that breakable objects, poisons, and other dangerous items are out of reach) is that your child has more of an opportunity to explore without danger.

As your child struggles to make decisions, it can be helpful to start simplistically talking with her about the different options and the consequences of each one. For example, Vicky had her bottle in one hand and reached for her sister's plastic cup with the other after her sister left the room. If her father said, "No. You have the bottle, and that cup is for your sister," the educational opportunity would be lost. Luckily, Vicky's father knew the importance of early decision making and said,

> Seems like you want both the bottle and the cup. Today you may hold both, but the bottle is for younger kids, and the cup

83

is for older kids. Let me get you another cup because that one is your sister's. You can try drinking a little bit of your milk in the cup. Let's see whether the bottle or the cup works best for you right now.

Initially, Vicky did not verbally respond and acted like she didn't hear her father's words. However, once her father gave her the new cup, she immediately smiled and dropped her bottle. She reached for the cup and said "Mine!" Vicky felt happy she had made one of her most important decisions up to this point! Although she sometimes still wanted the bottle, she made decisions based on her desire to be like her older sister or her desire to be comforted by the bottle when tired. Vicky's parents believed in saving the "No!" response for the dangerous and irreversible situations she might face. This parental philosophy allowed Vicky more room to explore her own decisions and the results of them.

During the toddler years, most children do not have a sense of long-term consequences. Clearly, they have not even been alive for long, so the word *long* can mean seconds or days in their minds. Focusing on their thinking, highlighting the decision-making process, and helping young children to make clear decisions and to be adaptable as well as flexible are important early skills to teach.

Decision Making During the Elementary School Years

By the time children reach elementary school, especially after the age of 7½, they have generally developed the *basic* cognitive ability to reason, consider consequences, try to persuade others to support their goals, and start to find solutions to some challenging situations. At this time, over-protective parents may communicate to their children the belief that the parent always knows best and the children should always ask what they should do before relying on their own thinking. Before children reach adolescence, it is crucial to help them develop decision-making and problem-solving skills before they "demand" more independence without the skills for it, including the recognition of consequences. During this period, here are a few key skills for children to learn.

CRITICAL THINKING SKILLS. By explaining the rationale behind your decisions, you can help children learn to use similar strategies. You can teach critical thinking skills needed for problem solving by

- talking with your child about how you thought about an issue and how you reached your decision (it is not always clear just by watching you in action);
- discussing how feelings are neither good nor bad, but decisions usually have to be determined by facts and consequences;
- discussing how learning to listen to a friend's opinions and goals can help your child to be more empathetic and open to viewing a situation differently (having this ability can also help your child to resolve conflicts in the friendship); and
- stressing how you use step-by-step thinking (similar to the ladder approach for goal setting described in Chapter 3) to reach decisions by breaking down the problem-solving plan into more manageable steps.

THE ABILITY TO COMPROMISE. Teaching children that it's sometimes important to be willing to accept less than what you want to get some of what you want. The following are some ways to teach this:

- Be willing to listen to your child's request so you can explain how you can use this information to create a compromise.

- When you compromise with your child, label it as such and highlight the fact that you are both giving up some of what you want to reach an agreement.
- If your child becomes frustrated and resistant and doesn't want to compromise, but you know it is the only way to give him a bit of what he wants, it's okay to give him time to consider the compromise before you have to say no to the entire request.
- Highlight that compromising with a friend can be difficult at first but can lead to a better relationship.

THE ABILITY TO WEIGH PROS AND CONS, INCLUDING SHORT-TERM AND LONG-TERM BENEFITS. In Chapter 3 you read about ways to help your child identify short-term and long-term goals. Knowing the goals is a key factor in decision making. Deciding between staying up late to watch a baseball game and being alert enough in the morning to take a big test creates a conflict between what your short-term and long-term goals are. Making the decision means thinking about which goal is more of a priority. The short-term goal for Eddie was to watch the game, but he wanted a good grade on the big math test so he reluctantly only watched half the game and recorded the rest to watch after the test.

The following are some strategies for helping children to weigh the pros and cons:

- Ask your child how he would feel immediately and then a few days after making a particular decision (e.g., watching the game but being too tired to do his best on the test).
- Encourage your child to think about the consequences of the decisions, not only for himself but also for friends, family, and others.
- Explain that sometimes the goal of keeping a friend is more important than the goal of always being right or having one's own way.

- Remind your child to think about what she needs to do now to reach her long-term goal later.

POSITIVE SELF-TALK. Have you ever been caught talking to yourself and felt embarrassed? Actually, talking to yourself can be productive. It can be done out loud when you are alone or quietly in your mind when you are in public situations. Although positive self-talk can be a useful tool, you may have a hard time convincing your child of this . . . at first.

Two very different kinds of self-talk are negative and positive. *Negative self-talk* occurs when people put themselves down or convince themselves they can't succeed or are inferior to others. For instance, when Phillip's friends were all trying out for the school play, Phillip told himself, "I can't do that. I'd just look stupid if I tried." Phillip used negative self-talk to convince himself not to try out for the play, and he missed the fun his friends had, even if they were just in the chorus. Conversely, *positive self-talk* can help people overcome difficult situations, gain confidence, and have the motivation to persevere when thinking of quitting a task.

The following are some ways to encourage your child to use positive self-talk:

- Model it by talking out loud (e.g., "I feel really good that I tried archery, even though I never did it before, not even as a kid! At first, I thought I would look foolish, but I would have felt foolish passing up the opportunity to learn").
- Discuss times when negative self-talk can do harm and positive self-talk can help (e.g., "There's no benefit to focusing on the fact that you did not get 100% on the test you studied for. Rather, you can feel proud that you studied and received a high grade, and you can learn from the questions you got wrong").

- Talk about how believing you "can't" makes the task more difficult, whereas believing you "can" (realistically) can boost motivation, confidence, and perseverance. Remember that just the simple apostrophe *t* (*can* vs. *can't*) can make the difference between believing and feeling defeated.

THE ABILITY TO CALM DOWN TO REACH SOUND DECISIONS. Many people, including adults, become passionate about an opinion or insistent on attaining a goal immediately. For example, 8-year-old Sean wanted to play the game Battleship with his friend even though his older brother was playing the game with his friend at that time. Sean asked for it. When that didn't work, he got upset and grabbed the game. His brother tried to take it back. The result was that the pieces went flying around the room and several were not able to be easily found. No one was able to play the game because of Sean's impulsive decision to grab it. When he'd calmed down, Sean admitted he did not use the best strategy that day. He liked the fact that he asked to play, at first. He knew that he could have waited for his brother to finish his game and then he would have been able to play. Sean also knew that there were other fun games he could have played with his friend. He felt that the problem would have been handled better if he was calm enough to make sound decisions.

The following are some ways to help children to calm down:

- Help them to realize that their loud talk, yelling, or tantrum delays them being heard rather than expediting it.
- Encourage them to identify when they are about to be impulsive (even kids can do this, even though they may not want to!).
- Teach them that when feeling impulsive, doing a "thinking task" may help calm them (e.g., count backward from 10, count backward by 7s from 100 for the math whiz, think about what they want to pack for their upcoming camping trip).

- Set a timer where no discussion will occur for the time pre-arranged (often 10 minutes is ample time).
- Set an example by appropriately verbalizing how you are handling your impulsive wishes in an adaptive way.
- Encourage breathing in slowly through the nose (as though taking in a sweet smell), then breathing out through the mouth (as though trying to cool down hot soup).

The Teenage Years: The Last Step Before Adulthood

When raising a child who will one day be an independent adult, be prepared to feel anxious at times during the teen years. After all, this is when they venture off on their own. During adolescence, many children begin to think about branching out and spending more time with friends, and they want to make more and more of their own decisions. Therefore, it is important now to let them more thoroughly think about ways to solve problems and to make advantageous rather than destructive decisions. You can be the sounding board, offering guidance when asked and nonjudgmental support. This way, they become more capable of relying on their own judgment, and you increasingly trust that judgment by the time they leave home.

Although the skill building you read about for supporting elementary school–aged children still applies here, let's talk about a few higher level skills to teach the teenagers . . . and how to do it!

FOSTERING DISCUSSIONS RATHER THAN ARGUMENTS. At this point, letting your child share, explore, evaluate, and sometimes rethink how she views problems and how she decides to respond are key to her minimizing impulsive decisions and picking ones that are best for the situation. In essence, you can view yourself as a guide and mentor. Sometimes family activities or situations allow your teen to be included in the decision making, with you right there to guide her. For instance, planning a vacation, choosing a new car, or trying to figure out how to get the best care for an ailing grandparent are all good opportunities to have your teen become part of the decision-making process.

Being a supportive mentor is not always easy. For instance, how would you handle the situation if your 16-year-old insists on going to a party where there will be no adult supervision? Be prepared for emphatic, repetitive insistence from your child: "I'm going. It's fine!" As parents, discussing rather than arguing involves

- pausing (don't feel pressured to respond immediately);
- calming yourself (so your child doesn't view you as simply reacting emotionally);
- being empathetic (remember how you felt at the same age, how important issues seemed, and how intense you felt about them back then);
- setting aside time to talk;
- listening;
- restating your child's point of view (e.g., if your child then says, "You just don't understand!" it might be helpful to calmly and honestly state, "No, I understand your point, I just don't agree with your conclusion");
- sharing why you believe it is not a good idea (if you still don't agree);
- listening again;
- seeing whether there's a compromise;
- discussing how it can hurt your child's goals, if you believe that is true (then say, "I understand why you want to go, but I can't agree to let you");

- if your child feels insulted that you don't trust her, explaining that because others will be at the party, you can't be sure you can trust those others to avoid setting up a concerning or even potentially dangerous situation;
- reminding your child of all the other times you deferred to her judgment and the potential serious consequences of agreeing to let her follow her desires on this particular occasion;
- if you find you have to set limits and disagree with your teenager, remember that you aren't her friend but rather her guide.

As your child gets older, you will likely have more situations in which you can compromise, so a time when you make a firm decision does not take away her independence overall.

Throughout the discussion, it is imperative (as you already probably know) to explain your rationale rather than criticize your child's thinking. Kids, and especially teenagers, who feel criticized or are concerned that they would disappoint their parents are often less comfortable sharing their thoughts, plans, and problems with an adult.

APPROPRIATE USE OF HUMOR. When trying to help your adolescent have discussions rather than arguments with you, carefully used humor is a valuable tool. However, when using humor, there is a fine line between appropriate humor and ridicule. Even when you use appropriate humor, your sensitive child may perceive it as ridicule, sarcasm, or minimizing his feelings. Therefore, it's important to think about your child and how using humor may or may not benefit the discussion and your relationship.

Appropriate humor often refers to the ability to make your point without lecturing. Appropriate humor is designed to bring the two of you together when just talking "at" each other is keeping you apart. The following is an example of appropriate use of humor:

Ian [age 15]: Dad, I want to drop out of school next year when I'm 16, and the law allows it.

Father: Sounds like a plan. What would you like to do?

Ian: [*Surprised at his father's response.*] I want to hitchhike across the country and see the sights with my friend Emily.

Father: Sounds exciting. Do you think Emily's parents will agree?

Ian: Probably not. If she doesn't go, I'll still have fun.

Father: Great. How will you pay your way?

Ian: Can't you pay? It's super educational!

Father: Ian, I'm 30 years older than you. If I'm going to pay for anyone to do that, it's me! [*This short bit of lighthearted humor can bond, not separate, the father and son.*] Seriously, you know that there's plenty of time for you to go on adventures later. I'm concerned about you sacrificing your education and your future goals for a one-time adventure. I would hate for you to want to get the high school diploma later and have to go back and get a GED or find other ways to get the credits.

Ian: So, wait. I can leave school at 16, but I won't have a diploma?

Father: That's right. You have to complete all the credits to get a diploma, and that usually

> takes 4 years. Even if you did summer
> school this year, you couldn't finish all the
> credits you need for a diploma.
>
> *Ian:* Oh. I didn't think about that. [*A few seconds go by.*] A road trip would have been
> a blast, though!
>
> *Father:* Yes, it would have been, and I would have
> loved to join you. It's just not practical.

In this example, you can see how respectful humor helped avoid an argument. Joseph's dad, however, yelled about how impractical, unrealistic, and spoiled Joseph was when Joseph brought up a similar idea. Their relationship was more stressed after the dialogue, whereas Ian felt closer to his father.

When you use humor, make sure your child feels you are being respectful of his or her feelings and being honest as you express your ideas and that you still address your child's thoughts and opinions. Sometimes humor is a good way to illustrate the impractical request of a teenager. For some adolescents, though, humor is never perceived as supportive in a discussion of their "wants." For these children, humor might have to be avoided to minimize the chance of it being misperceived.

ROLE-PLAY. Your teenager may not think that role-playing is a higher-level skill because young children engage in role-playing often as they use their imagination. However, at this stage, role-playing has a different goal and a different form. Role-playing can help teenagers as they continue to develop their perspective-taking and empathy-building skills.

Stephanie, age 14, came home and told her parents she was no longer going to talk to her former "BFF" (best friend forever) because her friend, Melanie, teased her about being a "bookworm" and a "nerd." Stephanie felt insulted and demeaned as well as surprised that a close friend would insult her. Stephanie's mother first acknowledged her daughter's feelings but then encouraged her to role-play the situation with her. Stephanie took on the role of Melanie while her mother took on Stephanie's role. The following is the dialogue and the insight that came from it:

> *Stephanie as Melanie:* You are such a bookworm. A super nerd.
>
> *Mom as Stephanie:* Ouch! That hurts coming from you. I thought we were friends.
>
> *Stephanie as Melanie:* Huh? Of course, we're friends. Don't you know a compliment when you hear one?
>
> *Mom as Stephanie:* That's no compliment I ever heard. It sounds like you are insulting me.
>
> *Stephanie as Melanie:* [*Paused, then said*] Maybe. Not sure. I didn't mean that. Maybe I'm a little jealous of how you spend so much time studying that I can't see you. And, of course, you get better grades than me.

Through this role-play, Stephanie was able to try to think about what her friend might have been thinking and feeling. Stephanie was no longer angry and was ready to have a real dialogue with Melanie. The next day, without being defensive, Stephanie talked with her friend. Melanie seemed surprised that Stephanie had been insulted; she thought she was simply being funny, but she then did acknowledge that she sometimes felt jealous of Stephanie's time studying and of her grades. They ended up having a better understanding of each other and continued their close friendship.

Another helpful form of role-playing you could consider trying with your teenager is role-reversal between the two of you. This can involve you asking your child to be you (the parent) while you take on her role (the child). When both parent and child do this seriously, your child may feel you truly understand his point of view, and you may find your child is better able now to understand your response.

There are times when role-playing can be helpful and other times when it is ill advised. For instance, when your child is emotional, it's a time to listen and be supportive and postpone the problem-solving exploration for later.

BRAINSTORMING SESSIONS. An individual can brainstorm ways to handle a situation. A team of people can join together to brainstorm and share more, and different, ideas. By letting your child know the family is like a team, stronger than any one member, she is less likely to feel defensive or concerned that you don't have faith in her problem-solving skills when you offer to help.

If you have been a brainstorming team member with your children in the early years, you will meet less resistance from them now when you try to work together to find the best solution to a situation or best way to reach a goal. If your children were given the opportunity to help you brainstorm how best to handle a situation you encountered when they were young (one that was appropriate to share with them, of course!), then they are more likely to realize that it is a sign of strength to brainstorm together.

Rarely is there only one road toward a given destination, but often there are quicker or more efficient ones. However, the quicker, more efficient paths are not always the best. Therefore, as you brainstorm, it is helpful to explore the potential consequences of each proposed plan.

In brainstorming sessions, model how you consider all the different options available. By thinking of more than one action or reaction, you are displaying divergent thinking. *Divergent thinking* is the ability to think of a variety of different ways to handle a given situation. The following are some tips for helping your child develop divergent thinking:

- While brainstorming, encourage your child to "think outside the box" (e.g., to be creative and try to find a variety of ways to solve problems).
- Though brainstorming is helpful for elementary school–aged children, it becomes even more important now when problems and decisions are more complicated and, at times, the actions can involve more negative consequences (e.g., whether to drop out of an activity, whether to get an after-school job, or if your child is open about the issue, what his attitude is about sex or using drugs).
- Help your child think about the best response so that he can reach his goals.
- Help your child to also think about how others (e.g., friends, relatives, teachers) would respond to her actions.
- Gently become more passive as your child develops more mature reasoning and decision-making skills in the brainstorming sessions.

"WHAT WOULD I DO?"

There is a brainstorming game that many children and teenagers have played with their families and enjoyed, called What Would I Do? It can be natural to engage in this game during car rides or during dinner conversations. The idea is to keep the conversation relaxed and allow all members of the family (even young children) to brainstorm how they would respond to a hypothetical situation. By making the situation hypothetical, no one has to feel pressured to make a decision that would affect one's life. However, by focusing on these hypothetical situations, it is possible to share ideas, focus on divergent ways of problem solving, and have fun at the same time. The following are a few ideas of scenarios for this game:

- What would you do if your friend asks you to give him your homework so he can copy it?
- What would you do if someone cuts in front of you as you are waiting to pay for a new pair of pants?
- What would you do if you discovered a unicorn in the woods? (Just a fun contemplation!)
- What would you do if your close friend tells you not to talk to another one of your friends and gives a vague explanation such as, "I don't like him?"

TIMELESS ADVICE FOR HELPING YOUR CHILD WITH DECISION MAKING

Respectfully expressing opinions opens the door to discussions. Remember when you were a child and disagreed with your parents' ideas or decisions? There may have been times when you didn't even listen to what your parents said because your message to them was really, "I am me, and you are you. I want to make my own decisions!" Even a toddler may try to express this idea, perhaps through actions rather than by using words. Of course, teenagers express this idea quite often!

When children communicate the message that they insist on handling situations in their own way, it can make parent–child discussions and explorations of options a bit of a challenge. Luckily, when your child is calm and not determined to block out your ideas, you have the opportunity to have those meaningful and productive conversations. During those moments, you might choose to list some of the natural consequences of the decision at hand, or you might choose to instead focus on the end goal.

The Power of Consequences

Children often work to please adults and avoid negative consequences. In decision-making conversations, you have the opportunity to help your child learn how to do this, as well as how to set his goals and work to reach them. If your child has successfully learned these lessons, it means that even if he doesn't want to do homework, he can consider the potential negative consequences of not doing the homework versus the long-term benefits of doing it. Usually, after weighing the pros and cons, confident children decide to choose, sometimes reluctantly, to do homework to work toward the long-term goal of being successful in class or getting into the honors program with friends.

Children do not always agree with parental advice. They are, at times, resistant to compromise. You have probably already encountered this. It can be frustrating when your child refuses to take your advice or follow your suggestions. If your child's plan is not appropriate or helpful but is also not dangerous, you may sometimes let the outside world provide the consequences.

Deon, for example, absolutely refused to do homework assignments in math, despite a discussion with his father about the potential consequences. Eventually, Deon's father shrugged his shoulders and said, "Okay, let me know how that works out for you." Shortly after that discussion, Deon was embarrassed in class when he found out he got zeros for all of his missed homework assignments and had to meet with his math teacher after class to talk about responsibility. When Deon's teacher called home, his father said, "Thank you for dealing directly with Deon about this. I'm trying to teach him that I'm not always going to stand between him and the consequences of the world."

Focusing on Goals

There are times when children focus on short-term goals rather than long-term goals (as discussed in Chapter 3). For instance, if a student does not like her teacher, she may make the decision to intentionally avoid doing work because her short-term goal is to punish the teacher for not being likable rather than focusing on her long-term goal of getting good grades to get into the college of her choice. Sometimes a child chooses to focus on the short-term goal of being with friends in a group chat rather than studying for a test. When long-term goals are derailed by the designated short-term goal, this can be problematic and worthy of a discussion between you and your child.

You have the opportunity to teach your child that the choices she makes in school, at home, and when interacting with her friends can all lead to either supporting or sabotaging her chances of reaching her goals. Children, even at a young age, are capable of learning that no matter how they feel about another person or a task, it does not have to derail them from doing what is ultimately best for reaching their goals.

SUMMARY

In this chapter, you had the opportunity to read about the importance of teaching children and adolescents effective decision-making and problem-solving skills to reach their goals. A variety of tips and techniques, for children of various ages, were revealed to help parents foster these abilities. In the next chapter, you will learn ways to help your children to develop frustration tolerance, another key ingredient in becoming an independent adult.

FRUSTRATION TOLERANCE: DEVELOPING YOUR CHILD'S PATIENCE AND ABILITY TO MANAGE OBSTACLES

Most parents become uncomfortable when their child appears to be emotionally suffering, unhappy, or disappointed. It is a natural instinct for loving parents to want to comfort their children immediately and relieve their stress. Unfortunately, a child who never experiences frustration, or learns the skill of patience, is a youngster who may not have the chance to develop coping strategies to deal with the world independently.

The good news is that there is no one right way to help your child to develop the ability to deal with stress and frustration. In this chapter, you will get the opportunity to explore many different ideas and strategies to support your child. You may already have some techniques you have successfully used.

Take a minute to reflect on how you react to your stressed child, and respond to the following statements. As you know, you won't be getting a grade, but, hopefully, this exercise will give you insight into your philosophy and how you are parenting.

For each item listed below, fill in the number that corresponds best to your response:

(continues)

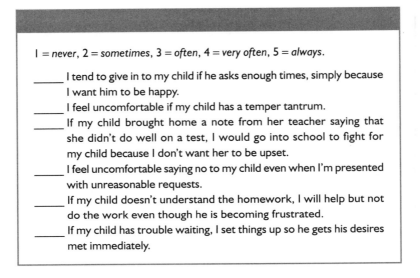

1 = *never*, 2 = *sometimes*, 3 = *often*, 4 = *very often*, 5 = *always*.

_____ I tend to give in to my child if he asks enough times, simply because I want him to be happy.

_____ I feel uncomfortable if my child has a temper tantrum.

_____ If my child brought home a note from her teacher saying that she didn't do well on a test, I would go into school to fight for my child because I don't want her to be upset.

_____ I feel uncomfortable saying no to my child even when I'm presented with unreasonable requests.

_____ If my child doesn't understand the homework, I will help but not do the work even though he is becoming frustrated.

_____ If my child has trouble waiting, I set things up so he gets his desires met immediately.

Now that you have completed the questionnaire, it's time to define *frustration tolerance*. Simply put, this term means that a person can handle being frustrated. Frustration is a feeling of annoyance, to varying degrees, when a person's desires are thwarted. A child (and even an adult) who can wait for the things that are attainable and tolerate the realization that some things will not be attained has the ability to tolerate frustration.

WHY ENDURE THE DISCOMFORT OF WAITING?

Every adult has experienced frustration at one time or another. Waiting for your new car to arrive at the dealership or waiting at the bus stop for a bus that is late during a blizzard both require patience. Having a tantrum when you have to wait would certainly bring stares and would not be productive.

If you can comfortably tolerate waiting and being patient, you will experience less of a sense of frustration and fewer feelings of being annoyed, angry, or even overwhelmed. Now, it's time to teach your child how to develop these skills to prevent him or her from feeling overwhelmed when wishes are not immediately granted or attained. Giving young children, and even teenagers, a chance to gradually build frustration tolerance can empower them for the rest of their lives. Frustration can start very young, and when this occurs, you have a great opportunity for a teachable moment.

The following are just a few examples of developmental frustrations and some environmentally produced opportunities for frustration:

- an infant or toddler has to wait sometimes to be fed;
- during toilet training, the toddler naturally has to feel the discomfort of briefly waiting to feel the pride of using the toilet;
- a teen who wants to reach puberty fast simply has to wait;
- a child who wants to be the star basketball player may need to accept limitations; and
- a child might need to ask questions and practice skills before feeling task mastery.

Throughout this chapter, we discuss ways parents can help children deal with both the developmental and the environmental frustrations of life.

DIFFERENT KIDS, DIFFERENT RESPONSES

You may have several children and help them build their frustration tolerance by reacting to them in different ways. This can be a sign of effective parenting. One child may accept a quick, calm "Not now, honey," whereas another child will argue with you until you can provide a logical reason or a reminder of the consequences of not being cooperative and accepting limits.

How do you know which response to give your child? Unfortunately, this is not an easy question to answer. Your child truly teaches you, over time, what works. However, the following are a few suggestions:

- Try quiet reasoning.
- Realize you don't have to explain everything in a hectic moment, but it helps to explain your parenting choices (not justify them!) later so your child understands.
- Remind your child of the potential consequences of desired or undesired actions (positive or negative consequences).
- Humor, if a child does not think he's being insulted, may be a good tactic for breaking an impasse.

The following are some quick examples of all four of the suggestions.

Use Quiet Reasoning

"We just spent a lot of money on our family vacation. I'm afraid you will have to wait until we can get you your new bike."

Explain When You Have More Time

When you are rushed, you could say something like, "I know you want to talk more about the possibility of you getting a bike. Right now, we're rushing to pick up your sister. Let's talk tonight after dinner." But remember to keep your appointment. If you promise to talk, it's seen as a verbal contract and a trust issue if you don't keep that appointment. When you have time to talk, you could say, "I know you were frustrated when I said we can't afford the bike right now. Dad and I want you to have the bike.

Let's brainstorm on how you can earn money to help pay for it." This discussion is beneficial because it shows your child that you can compromise and he can take some responsibility to work toward a goal.

Remind Your Child of Consequences

Many parents dread the time when their child insists on doing something or getting something, and they do not approve. Children frequently have many strategies to help them convince you (e.g., nagging, begging, tantrums). Now it's your time to develop your own strategies. Here are a few:

- Be consistent.
- Restate what your child's wish is so he knows he was heard ("I understand that you want _____, but I do not agree"). Understanding and agreeing are not synonymous.
- Try to remain calm.
- Avoid discussing the issue when your child is emotionally unavailable to hear you. However, remind her you will talk once she is calm.
- Acknowledge that it's hard sometimes to be frustrated.
- You don't always have to compromise—you can make some decisions guilt-free!
- Discuss consequences. Your child may want a play date before doing homework. The consequences (e.g., being too tired to do the work well or not having time to finish) can be highlighted as well as your family rule of work before play. The consequence of your child listening may be a good mark on the homework and feeling more confident in class the next day.
- Discussing possible consequences may not matter to your child at the moment. If you find that your child is resistant, you can

explain that cooperation is important for any family. The more cooperative your child is, the less stressed and more responsive you can be because you are not exhausted from the battles.

Use Humor

This strategy can backfire if your child feels you are using sarcasm and laughing at him. However, humor can also connect people and can disarm a child who is prepared for arguments. It's a great tool for kids to learn for their future use as well. The following is an example of a parent using humor to avoid an argument.

Evan didn't want to go to school one morning. He wanted to stay home and play with his new puppy. His mother responded, "Great idea! I will even write a note to the teacher saying, 'Evan stayed home from school today because he didn't want to go. Rather, he preferred to stay home and play with our new puppy.' Of course, you will have to deal with the teacher tomorrow. Good luck!" Evan, realizing that his mother was not challenging him as she smiled and wished him good luck, felt freer to weigh the pros and cons of staying home. He decided to go to school and play with his puppy later.

If your child doesn't feel challenged and simultaneously knows you are not laughing at him, there is less for him to argue about. Therefore, he may be open to thinking through the situation on his own or to accept your input as a supportive guide.

DIFFERENT SITUATIONS, DIFFERENT RESPONSES

As you probably already realize, not all children require the same responses, and not all situations warrant the same reaction. One important differentiation for parents to make before responding to their child's requests is, is it a need or a want?

A mother, for example, who sought help from a local therapist complained that her daughter was "spoiled." She later commented, "My daughter is going to college, and she said she needs new sweaters before she leaves." When asked how many sweaters her daughter had, she said, "Twelve or 13." Do you think this woman's daughter needed or simply wanted the sweaters? Would you have purchased new sweaters for your daughter in this situation? There is no easy answer. The following are a few things to consider:

- Are the sweaters warm enough for the area where your daughter will be attending college?
- Were you planning on spending a certain amount for the college transition, and after discussing how to spend the money, your daughter sacrificed in other areas to get the sweaters?
- Are her sweaters old and worn out?
- Does your daughter rarely ask for materialistic items and, therefore, you want to fulfill this wish?

The request (e.g., asking for the sweaters) may be a want of a "spoiled" child or may be simultaneously both a want and a need. That's what makes parenting so difficult. Each situation presents different factors and possible solutions. However, this can make parenting interesting!

Sometimes, of course, wants are just wants, and parents have to decide whether they will give in to their child's request in order to be a popular parent because they don't want their child to feel frustrated or because they simply think it's a fun and good idea. Sometimes, though, there is a clear need and a clear reason to grant your child's request in a timely manner.

Most parents have experienced a crying child who seems to need something quickly or urgently. At times, a child's cries are a sign of danger, and he truly needs your immediate response. For instance, 9-year-old Isaac had hypoglycemia. When he cried out to his mother that he needed his orange juice, she knew him well enough to realize he was reacting to a potentially dangerous medical situation. If he did not raise his blood sugar level, the consequence could have been serious. If your 3-year-old cries that he needs to "go potty," this becomes another urgent situation because your child is asking to avoid an accident. Luckily, few situations require such immediate responses by parents.

CHILDREN'S AGE AND HOW IT AFFECTS YOUR RESPONSES

As young as infancy, children start their journey toward developing frustration tolerance. For example, even a few minutes of waiting to be fed or cleaned or burped (to relieve gas) can be uncomfortable for a newborn.

A child's age plus whether he is an only child or fitting into a family with siblings all may affect how quickly parents can respond. Do you ever feel you are being neglectful when your child cries and you have to split your time between several children? Rather than neglect, this is often more a feeling of guilt on the part of parents. A chronically deprived youngster or a child who consistently is kept from getting basic needs or emotional care is a child who is neglected. Interestingly, a child who is never given the opportunity to develop frustration tolerance is deprived in this narrow area of development.

When older children have not developed the ability to tolerate frustration, they may find that life is stressful as they try to cope with having to wait or accept limitations that can typically arise in teenage and adult years. For instance, when a 13-year-old seems to be consistently unable to tolerate an unexpected 10-minute delay in being driven to a friend's house or a 17-year-old feels angry and depressed after learning that he can't pick the family's meal for that evening, it signals that both adolescents are struggling to develop their frustration tolerance.

To help your child develop frustration tolerance, let's review the different reactions you might consider depending on your child's age and the given situation. When a toddler starts to cry because of a dirty diaper, you want to attend to her discomfort quickly because you want to have her associate the relief of cleanliness with a later motivation to be toilet trained rather than getting used to the irritation of the dirty diaper. However, if a toddler cries that he wants to leave the pediatrician's office before being seen, this is a different kind of frustration, warranting a different reaction.

Toddlers often communicate behaviorally, and crying is one such behavior. If your child is fearful, comfort is essential. If the toddler is bored, it's okay to provide this child with choices for filling the time (e.g., offering several fun toys for your child to select from). This will let your child know that he has to tolerate the boredom of the environment but can have coping strategies (e.g., toys) that aren't fully organized by you! Developing a way to cope with impatience or frustration in a teenager starts at a very young age.

The world outside your home is filled with times of excitement, but it is also filled with periods of frustration. The elementary school–aged child has many opportunities to experience frustration. The use of the word *opportunities* in the previous sentence may seem odd. However, some periods of frustration really are opportunities for growth and preparation for the future. Earlier in this chapter, you read some examples that pertain to your child at home. The following are some further examples of how opportunities for frustration can occur in a variety of settings for your child:

- At home, a child knows he has to do his homework before playing.
- A child calls a friend for a play date and learns that the friend is busy.
- A child loves soccer but didn't make the "A," or travel, team.
- A child wants a toy or video game that is inappropriate for her age.

Because life presents your child with these teachable moments, it's a great time to help her learn coping strategies for waiting. The following is an example of lessons taught by a parent.

Katie's father knew her crying and shouting prevented her from effectively and quickly dealing with being frustrated. After consulting the school psychologist for guidance, he helped 10-year-old Katie practice some calming strategies in moments when she was not frustrated. Katie learned

- that crying and shouting can exhaust her without her intended goal being met;
- that she and her father could have fun creating some ways to help her calm down so that she could feel less overwhelmed;
- to focus on slowly breathing in (like smelling newly baked brownies) and then breathing slowly out (like trying to move a feather a few inches on a table);
- that "not now" does not always mean "not ever";
- to use positive self-talk, such as, "I survived not being in class with my BFF, and it turned out fine, so I know I can deal with in a different skating group than she is now";

- that self-talk can help her focus on her strengths, laugh with herself, and be her own best cheerleader and supporter when frustrated; and
- that talking calmly with her parents can often lead to a feeling of not being alone and, at times, may even lead to a compromise.

Songs often include strong messages that can apply to everyday life without being critical. For instance, Katie and her father spent some enjoyable time searching through their favorite music lyrics for examples of ways to deal with frustration. After her father introduced her to one of his favorite songs from the Rolling Stones, "You Can't Always Get What You Want," father and daughter talked about how it dealt with the fact that it's possible to deal with frustration and disappointment. Next, Katie loved having her father listen to one of her favorite songs by Taylor Swift titled "Shake It Off" on YouTube and hearing how her father felt it also applied to the same concept. Not only was this a fun exploration of how others, even famous musicians, know about disappointments but it was also a great experience for both father and daughter to share something from each generation with the other.

Eventually, your toddler becomes an older child, then a tween, and then a teenager. Hopefully, by the time you are raising an adolescent, the skills described earlier will have been learned to a great extent. In the teen years, children are working to gain more control of their lives and often develop great debating skills (which sometimes may exhaust you!). However, they may also revert to more childlike coping strategies such as "I want what I want when I want it."

Many parents have felt exasperated when trying to help teenagers accept limits and frustration. Adolescents may have debating skills but seem to be simply arguing and accusing adults of causing them unnecessary stress. If a parent argues back, the teen often just escalates. The following are some quick tips for helping your adolescent deal with the frustration that comes with having to accept limits:

- A parent can calmly say, "This arguing is not getting us anywhere. Let's talk about options we can both agree on. Maybe we can find a good compromise."
- Parents don't have to come up with an immediate response. It's okay to tell your teenager that you understand the request, but you need time to think about it.
- Rephrase what your child wants, so he knows you heard him, then ask him to restate your position after you share it.
- Explain logically why you made your decision.

Not all children develop at the same rate, so you may find that some of the strategies for teenagers are appropriate for your child at a much younger age. Similarly, some adolescents can benefit from strategies you read about for younger children. One of the challenges of being a parent is to tailor your responses to each of your children's ages and developmental levels because your children are likely to act and react differently from each other.

IMMEDIATE VERSUS DELAYED GRATIFICATION

You don't have to be a child to want immediate gratification. Have you ever indulged in an enticing dessert despite being on a diet because you "wanted it"? Or, perhaps you engage in impulse buying. Adults and kids are not that different after all!

Your child or teenager, like you, isn't necessarily spoiled just because she wants something *now*. However, if she feels she can't deal with the frustration of waiting, she is at a disadvantage in dealing with life's challenges as she grows up.

A study worth noting is one that was done at Stanford University in the 1960s and 1970s. It is often referred to as "The Marshmallow

Test." In this study, preschool-aged children were placed in a room, one at a time. The evaluator presented each child with a marshmallow (or another desired item) and explained that the child could eat it then or wait until the evaluator returned and get an additional marshmallow (or another item). Some children ate the marshmallow quickly, whereas others waited to double the reward. In the longitudinal study, the evaluator, Walter Mischel, kept track of these children over time. He discovered some important results: Those who waited were more successful in their teen and adult lives (see the Suggested Readings list at the back of this book for more information).

Waiting and surviving the frustration can help a child feel self-confident and decrease anxiety and being overwhelmed by having to deal with delaying gratification. In some interesting way, then, helping your child cope with delayed gratification is an important gift! Yet, it can cause conflict for parents who don't want their child to be frustrated.

There are many situations in which a child has to wait. In school, students may have to wait until their lunch period to tell a great story to a friend. Kids generally have to work on skills before reaching their goals of being a star athlete or a finalist in a school spelling bee.

There are times when "maybe" or "later" might be your answer to your child's request. Parents sometimes put enormous pressure on themselves to give immediate answers to avoid a disappointed or angry child. It is okay to say, "Let me think about it" or "We can't talk about this right now." It is also okay to let your child pout or be angry with you. If you have a strong relationship, this delayed response should not permanently cause a rift. There will be times when you don't want to say yes or no but find a compromise. The following are two examples.

Isabella, age 13, wanted the latest iPhone and said, "I can't live without it. All my friends are getting one." Her parents spoke about it with each other and decided to say, "We know your old phone is antiquated, so we'll chip in half." At first, Isabella was disappointed that her parents weren't immediately paying for and giving her the phone. Isabella and her parents then discussed why this compromise was appropriate and ways that Isabella could earn her portion of the new phone. Following this talk, Isabella understood her parents' reasoning and was willing to start earning money for the phone. Her parents realized they were giving Isabella not only a phone but also a sense of financial responsibility, ability to delay gratification, and pride in earning her money.

Johnny, age 11, wanted to go to a 2-week basketball summer camp. His father said,

> I love that you put in a lot of time shooting baskets. I think you need to put some of that energy into your math work. If you go for extra help in school and work hard on your math, no matter what grade you get, then you can go to the camp.

Because the ability to wait and tolerate frustration is key to becoming a functional adult, it's important to give your child the opportunity to experience and face these feelings. This may be difficult or even painful because you aren't immediately gratifying your child's wishes, but it will benefit her in the long run. Of course, have fun enjoying the smile when you sometimes give her that immediate gratification!

WHAT'S WRONG WITH PROTECTING MY CHILD FROM EMOTIONAL PAIN?

Many adults feel that protecting children from physical harm and emotional pain are their main responsibilities. Without adults who protect them, young children would die from starvation or exposure to cold, and so forth. Therefore, the instinct to protect the young (which many in the animal kingdom display!) is necessary and not to be downplayed here.

There is a delicate balance between protection and overprotection. Overprotection can be viewed as deprivation. Confusing? If parents protect their children from any and all frustration, any healthy risks (e.g., trying to ride a bicycle or learn to ice skate), or any need to delay gaining what they want (e.g., a day off from school to play video games even though school is in session), the children may be deprived of the chance to gain the frustration tolerance so important in developing a healthy, confident life. The following are some examples of when parents felt they were being caring, yet unintentionally deprived their child of the chance to face an emotional challenge.

Olivia, age 7, was the only girl her age who was not allowed to ride her bicycle without the training wheels. Her parents felt that they were protecting her from being injured by falling off the bike. Olivia interpreted their actions as, "My parents think I can't ride like the other kids. They're probably right. I don't want to ride anymore. Riding around with training wheels is way too embarrassing."

Mitchell, age 10, wanted to try out for the school play. His parents reminded him that it would take a lot of time away from his other activities and that he would have lots of lines to memorize. They were worried their son would feel tense, and they were concerned about adding stress to his life. Rather than seeing his parents' response as supportive, Mitchell's enthusiasm disappeared because he felt his parents did not have confidence that he could juggle this added responsibility.

Jack, age 11, was upset when he found out that he was in class with a few friends, but not his best friend. His mother tried to calm her son and promised to go to his school and talk to the principal about changing his class. Jack was moved into the class with his friend but didn't have the opportunity to learn he could deal with this separation and the frustration of not getting his "ideal" class situation.

How do you know whether you are overprotecting your child? It's not always easy to figure this out. As you read earlier in this chapter, each child and each situation can be different and call for a different level of protection, nurturance, and support. It is a judgment call. The following are a few things to consider:

- Is there a dangerous, rather than a healthy, risk to not protecting your child? If so, protect her (even if she is frustrated by your action).
- Is the danger potentially permanent (e.g., death)? Definitely intervene!
- Are you communicating "You can do it!" by not intervening when there is a healthy risk? Then stand by and be supportive, but don't take over and intervene.
- Can you intervene by helping your child figure out how she can handle the situation on her own, despite the fact that she wants you to "fix it" for her?

If you want to keep your child from any frustration, just remember that you want to eventually have an adult child who is competent to manage the stresses of life. If you start teaching this lesson early, you are protecting her by helping her build up her coping skills and self-confidence to deal with anxiety-producing situations (e.g., interviewing for a job), anger, impatience, and so forth.

POPULAR PARENT VERSUS EFFECTIVE PARENT

How many parents do you think want to be loved by their children? Clearly, the answer is almost all or all. However, sometimes parents want that unconditional love so much they make decisions that lead to the child smiling and saying, "You're the best!" even when the decision made by the parent is not truly the best for that child. Saying yes keeps a child from being disappointed but also keeps that child from realizing she can survive times of frustration. As you have already read, learning to cope with frustration is important as any child grows into the teen years and then into adulthood.

Many children seem to know what words can hurt a parent, undermine a parent's confidence, and lead to guilt. Have you ever heard a child (maybe even your own) say, "You are the worst parent!" or "I hate you!" or roll his eyes in a dramatic manner? Clearly, you don't want your child to react consistently to you like this or believe these words. However, the words may be masking the message, "Can't you make my world fun and easy? Why are you making me deal with waiting for what I want or not getting something I had hoped for?" This may be a discussion worth having with some mature children, but not in a tense moment.

There is a big difference between your child's temporary anger at you and truly hating you. If you hear the strong words, it's okay to think about what he's saying and think about why you are sticking to your decision. If you think your child's point is valid, it's okay to take a moment and then compromise or even change your mind. Changing your mind only because you want to be the popular parent is different from changing your mind because your child has given you a logical argument or reason for you to do so.

DECIDING WHEN TO GIVE IN AND WHEN TO SAY NO

Now that you have read about the dangers of overprotection and making decisions so you can be the popular parent, there are still many times when it is okay to give in to your child's requests. It might be helpful to think of these situations as times when you are simply agreeing with your child rather than giving in.

When your child makes a request, sometimes your response seems easy and leads your child to think you are the best parent in the whole world. For instance, Will wanted to have a play date with his friend sometime during the weekend. Because he finished his school project and had free time, his parents said, "Absolutely!" One key point, however, that his parents did not share was the rationale behind their agreement. Sometimes children think a parent's decision is random. Will's parents might consider sharing their thinking in the future so their son understands why they sometimes say yes and sometimes say no. He will learn there is a rational thought process involved.

There are times when your initial reaction to your child's request is to say no. Is it okay to change your mind? Some parents fear it is a sign of weakness to recant, even after their child presents a logical and rational argument. If this happens to you, realize you are probably modeling flexibility and not indecisiveness. Parents can use the following thought process as a guide:

- If the situation is dangerous, no is your only response even if your child argues or is frustrated.
- If you say no to a situation that is not dangerous, try to share your rationale so your child eventually can model how to think rationally and make a decision (the younger the child, the fewer words in your response). Share your rationale at a time when your child is calm so she can absorb what you are saying.
- If you say no to a situation that is not dangerous, but you want to set limits, think about whether your child has to take on a task before you can say yes (e.g., "Do your homework before

you play the video game") to teach him to delay gratification and meet his responsibility.

- If you can't find a good reason to say no, consider your child's respectful, logical argument and then say yes. This can teach your child a sense of confidence in her ability to critically look at a situation and communicate clearly.

As you consider whether to say yes or no, remember that sometimes saying no leads to frustration on the part of your child. Remember, frustration isn't always a negative thing. If you have a clear conviction as to why you are saying no, feel free to absolve yourself of guilt or anxiety and remind yourself that you are preparing your child to survive frustration and some deprivation in life.

HELPING YOUR CHILD FEEL SPECIAL (BUT NOT THE CENTER OF THE UNIVERSE)

When newborns enter the world, they seem to simply lie around, giggle, or cry, and hopefully find that their discomforts are quickly fixed, and their comforts are plentiful. For the first few months of life, life is a wonderment when an adult magically appears and takes care of all needs. The newborn is hopefully fed, cleaned, coddled, and cherished. Not a bad life, huh?!

Imagine being 20 years old and lying around hoping that all desires are met instantly. Not a good thing, right? How do we help the infant turn into a healthy and independent 20-year-old? If the 20-year-old feels he is the center of the universe and everyone should put his requests and needs above all else, this is a young person who is ill prepared for the realities of the world. This person also has not learned the confidence that comes from realizing he can survive frustration.

The age at which a child begins to learn he or she is not the center of the universe can depend on environmental factors (e.g., having to sit in a car seat, school expectations), physical factors (e.g., toilet training), social factors (e.g., having to share a toy or compromise to keep a friend), and family factors (e.g., birth of a sibling, a family obligation).

How do you help your child feel special yet not the center of the universe? If children are raised to be protected from all frustration, difficulties, and obstacles, they won't be given opportunities to learn to deal with these experiences as they get older and more expectations are placed on them. Therefore, the parents who believe they are giving everything to their "center of the universe" are depriving that child of the ability to gradually learn to cope as a member of the universe or community.

TIPS FOR RESPONDING TO TEMPER TANTRUMS AND TEARS

Have you ever noticed that you quickly change your plan of action when you notice your child is about to start crying or have a temper tantrum? Many parents, especially when this happens in a public setting, just want to avoid their child engaging in these actions and will give in, withdraw from the situation, or feel helpless and embarrassed.

Tantrums Are a Type of Communication

Temper tantrums can occur at any age. You may even have seen adults having full-blown temper tantrums when they are frustrated. Of course, a toddler's temper tantrum requires a different response from a temper tantrum of an adolescent or an adult.

Toddlers have complicated desires without sophisticated language to communicate them to you. Some young children also have articulation difficulties so they are not easily understood, others have language delays, and some have simply learned that having a tantrum leads to their parents giving them what they want.

Although many parents become uncomfortable or even angry about tantrums, if you think about toddler tantrums as a rudimentary means of communication, it may be easier for you to keep your cool and help your child through this emotional reaction. Once calm, it's time to start building the ability to communicate without the tantrum.

For instance, while Nadine was having a tantrum, her mother sat by quietly, making sure she was safe but not engaging in a dialogue. This approach is often more difficult for parents to stick to when the tantrum happens in a public place. During her tantrum, in the family's living room, Nadine kept saying, "I want pagetti, I want pagetti." Her mother just calmly said, "We'll talk when you are ready." Nadine soon tired of her crying and flailing and was ready to talk. Her mother then said, "I would love to give you spaghetti, but we have none in the house. When I go shopping next, I'll make sure to buy some. Let's go look at the food we have and see whether we can find something you would like to eat now." Nadine cuddled with her mother for a few minutes and felt understood.

Now, let's think about 14-year-old Nadine having a similar tantrum after her parents explained they would have loved to buy the outfit she wanted, but it was too expensive, and they couldn't afford it. Nadine screamed, called her parents many unflattering names, kicked the wall, stormed up to her room, and slammed the door. What would you have done if you were Nadine's parent? The sense of helplessness parents can feel in this situation is not uncommon. However, are parents truly helpless in this kind of a situation? The following are a few things to consider if you are ever in this predicament:

- Children sometimes yell and fight to do something, knowing that the parent will still say no. Sometimes these children are secretly relieved when their parents do not give in and instead stick to their original response (the children don't have to do something they really didn't want to do, yet they can tell their friends they would have done it, but their parents wouldn't let them).
- In the moment of the tantrum, telling your child she is being rude or disrespectful can escalate the anger and distract from the issue causing the tantrum (there is always time later to discuss this).
- You could try, although you may not always be heard, to tell your child that there are more effective ways to express anger (and model it for your child every time you are upset). Sometimes this conversation is better received once your child has calmed down.
- When your child can listen, explain your rationale regarding why you are insisting on saying no (e.g., the potential negative consequences of letting your child do what is wanted).
- Be prepared for glares, anger, tears, and hurtful comments, but try to remember that you have a strong relationship (if this is true), the tantrum will eventually end, and the learning moment can then begin.

If you do not trust that you and your child have a close parent–child relationship, and most of your time is spent "putting out fires," you can consult with a mental health professional who can guide you or work with your family to improve the relationship. In addition, spending family time doing activities during which everyone laughs, has fun, and creates fond memories can do wonders for bringing children and parents together.

Tears Without Tantrums

Children may express their frustration with not getting what they want by crying. Unlike the anger that some parents experience when their child has a tantrum, parents may react with guilt when seeing their child upset and in tears. When a child is in tears, he sometimes seems inconsolable, whereas other times he is just teary. The seemingly inconsolable child needs your support and acknowledgment of his pain, even if you don't change your mind. Through his tears, he may say, "You don't understand at all!" A suggested response to this frequent statement is, "I understand that . . . [be specific]. I just don't agree that you should . . . [be specific]." If your child is a teenager who is in tears, you can say, "I understand, but understanding and agreeing are not synonymous."

MODELING HOW YOU HANDLE FRUSTRATION

Although some children are hesitant to admit it, they watch and learn from the actions and words of their parents. Many children are fascinated by stories one parent tells another about how a conflict or problem was dealt with. In fact, talking directly to children about how to handle a situation may not be nearly as effective as having them "eavesdrop" on a conversation you are having with another adult about how you handled frustration.

Whether someone sneaks into line ahead of you at the grocery store or cuts you off as you drive on the highway or whether you tried to get tickets to see your favorite music group only to learn the concert was sold out, use the real-life frustration as a real-life example if it's age appropriate to share with your child. There are probably many times when you are with your child when you can model how you handle frustration.

SUMMARY

Now that you have read through the important ways of helping your child gain the ability to manage frustration and be more patient, you may want to periodically refer back to this chapter as your child grows and presents you with new challenges. You may also want to revisit your answers to the questionnaire at the start of this chapter to see whether you have changed any of your opinions or responses.

From now on, if your child is upset with you when you do not always give in to requests, remind yourself that you are preparing your child for life. Having the ability to handle frustration, at times, can improve your child's chances of being successful in school, socially, when working toward goals, and eventually in his or her job.

CHAPTER 6

SELF-MONITORING: TEACHING YOUR CHILD TO LOOK WITHIN

At all stages, when your children are separating from you, they have the opportunity to practice self-monitoring skills. For young children, sleeping at a relative's home can involve a degree of self-monitoring, despite having relatives around to care for and support them. For instance, a child who self-monitors can often use all the social skills learned at home (e.g., "please" and "thank you") because that child is monitoring his behavior and wants to appear polite to his relatives.

As your child gets older and ventures off to places such as sleep-away camp and, later, college, she will need self-monitoring skills to avoid impulsive actions and to make sound decisions. There are many parents who become anxious when their grown children go off to college because they fear their children may not monitor their behaviors, may not always go to class, and may indulge in certain potentially dangerous activities (e.g., drinking, drugs, promiscuity).

Before continuing in this chapter, take a minute to reflect on how you encourage your child to self-monitor and to accept the consequences of his or her actions.

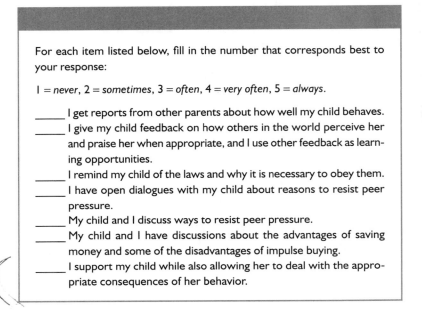

For each item listed below, fill in the number that corresponds best to your response:

1 = *never*, 2 = *sometimes*, 3 = *often*, 4 = *very often*, 5 = *always*.

_____ I get reports from other parents about how well my child behaves.

_____ I give my child feedback on how others in the world perceive her and praise her when appropriate, and I use other feedback as learning opportunities.

_____ I remind my child of the laws and why it is necessary to obey them.

_____ I have open dialogues with my child about reasons to resist peer pressure.

_____ My child and I discuss ways to resist peer pressure.

_____ My child and I have discussions about the advantages of saving money and some of the disadvantages of impulse buying.

_____ I support my child while also allowing her to deal with the appropriate consequences of her behavior.

WHAT SELF-MONITORING IS . . . AND ISN'T

In a society with so many cameras, what is happening and how people are acting are constantly being monitored. Rather than you or "society" having to monitor and respond to your child's actions, wouldn't it be great if he took responsibility for doing this for himself? Self-monitoring is not only about working to avoid punishment or negative consequences. Self-monitoring is not necessarily about doing things to please others, although sometimes that is important. It is not even only about wanting to please one's mother and father or agree with all their ideas. People who self-monitor can feel good about their choices and themselves. By self-monitoring, your child is less likely to feel embarrassed when "caught" doing something impulsive and more likely to make decisions that help build up his reputation and self-pride.

TEACHING YOUR CHILD HOW TO SELF-MONITOR

Because it is unlikely that you will be around your child all day, every day, to tell her what to do, what not to do, and how others view her based upon her choices, it's imperative that she learn to self-monitor. If you could be around your child all day long and monitor everything she does, she may not get the chance to learn the value of monitoring herself and how to do this.

Self-monitoring is learned gradually and not expected from an infant. Over time, children learn how to self-monitor from the guidance of parents, the reactions others have to their actions, and from watching how others interact with the world around them. There are beneficial ways to guide children to monitor their behaviors.

Talk With Your Children About the Image They Want to Present to Others

Many young children and even teenagers often react impulsively to situations and don't instinctively spend time thinking about the consequences of their actions and how they might affect themselves and others. Creating an attainable image of how they want to be perceived by their friends, teachers, and members of their community can be used as a goal and a guide.

Danny, for instance, grew up in a rural neighborhood. He was one of the few children in it who practiced his particular religion. He was often misunderstood and sometimes teased because he was in the religious minority. His mother told him, "Danny, when you go out in the world, you not only represent yourself but also our whole family, and you teach others about who people of our religion are and about our values." From an early age, Danny felt the need to self-monitor because of his mother's words and his pride in representing both his family and his religion.

Self-monitoring to represent family, religion, race, or another group is difficult for some children who fear or even experience teasing by peers because of their strong commitment to family values. However, with a close parent–child bond and simultaneous parental monitoring to make sure your child isn't being bullied, your child will be more likely to withstand peer pressure and gain a sense of personal satisfaction.

There are different ways to talk about self-monitoring with your child. Bobby's father told him, "If I ever get a report from anyone that you were disrespectful or broke any rules, you'll be in big trouble." Bobby, at the age of 11, interpreted his father's words to mean, "I can do what I want, but I better be careful not to get caught." His father's threats plus the fact that he was not taught how to self-monitor led him to make some decisions without considering how his actions would affect his goals and consequences. What Bobby did learn were ways to hide some of his behaviors from his father rather than feeling he could turn to his father to figure out how to learn from errors and make more positive choices.

If Bobby's father had said, "I will not always be around you. Let's talk about your decisions and how you feel about them now that you know how they affect your reputation and the reputation of others," Bobby might have seen his father as a mentor and not as an adversary. How do you think the different parenting approaches affected Bobby when he went to college and had to self-monitor?

Each individual, whether young or old, wants to see himself in a certain way. You can help guide your child as he forms his self-image. A confident child who feels closely connected to, and valued by, a support team often strives for a positive self-image. The following are a few questions to help your child consider what her image is and how she feels about it:

- What reputation do you hope to have with friends? What have you done to achieve this? Is there a risk in forming that reputation (e.g., "brainless jock," "tough kid," "BFF to everyone," "studious student")?
- What reputation do you hope to have with teachers? What have you done to achieve this? Is there a risk in forming that reputation (e.g., "class clown," "the one who always does everything right")?
- What reputation do you want to have for yourself? How do you feel about your reputation (e.g., Are you proud of yourself? Do you feel good about yourself when you look in the mirror? Can you name three positive attributes that describe yourself?)? If your child is not proud of her reputation, you can go back to the earlier chapters and set short- and long-term goals that focus on achieving a more positive self-image and reputation.

Pride (having it or seeking it) is an essential element in guiding one's behavior. Not having pride, having false pride (bravado), or having a lack of confidence can lead people to lower their expectations for themselves and allow them to make choices that don't raise their self-esteem.

Lizzy, age 12, preferred hanging out with friends, going on bike rides, and playing video games rather than studying and doing her homework. When she received low test grades, she hid them from her friends because she was embarrassed and felt "stupid." She ended up with a self-fulfilling prophecy of believing she couldn't do well in school, not trying, and then not doing well and getting poor grades.

Lizzy's mother spoke with her daughter about how ashamed Lizzy felt of herself. They had an honest, nonjudgmental discussion about how Lizzy had truly not tried and how her grades did not reflect on her actual ability. They set a list of Lizzy's priorities, including being proud of herself rather than ashamed of her grades, studying, doing homework, and continuing to have some fun time.

Lizzy's parents and guidance counselor coached her in developing executive functioning skills (see Chapter 3), Lizzy met weekly with her teacher for extra help before school, and even set up a study group with two friends. Lizzy was excited about the possibility that she could develop pride in her work ethic and school grades. Her grades improved, and her pride in her academic competence led her to work even harder!

Talk With Your Child About Peer Pressure

As you probably know, being accepted by one's friends becomes much more important to your child when she hits adolescence. However, peer pressure is often noticed even when a child is in preschool or elementary school. Kiersten came home from elementary school and told her father she urgently needed to get a special doll because her best friend in school had one. Kiersten not only liked the doll but also felt it was important to have one to fit in with her friend.

In elementary school, many children join certain activities, such as signing up to play a particular sport, to be with the popular kids even if they don't love the experience. Others start to dress in a certain fashion that is considered cool by peers. Because you are not always around your child, and the peer group is often gaining influence when you are not there (e.g., school, extracurricular activities, parties), it is important for your child to carry your values wherever she goes and self-monitor so she makes healthy choices.

During the teenage years, the pressure to fit in with one's friends and peers may lead your children to behave in ways that allow them to conform to their peers. These behaviors are not always in their best interest or representative of the values you had earlier instilled in them. During adolescence, children can also be less communicative with parents. This combination of changes in behavior and less openness in discussions can cause many parents to feel anxious and concerned.

A certain amount of rebellion in adolescence and independent thinking in children is normal and healthy. It shows that children are trying to become individuals and not just clones of their parents. However, if your child does not self-monitor, the rebellion or independent thinking can lead to risky, counterproductive, or even destructive decisions.

There are ways to help children self-monitor, even when they face peer pressure. The following are a few tips:

- When watching a family TV show, there are many times when the theme is peer pressure. During a commercial break or after the program has ended, talk about this topic because children are less defensive when talking about peer pressure that does not directly affect them.
- Say to your child, "You don't have to tell me, but be honest with yourself. Do you really approve of how your friends are behaving?"
- Ask some of the questions posed earlier in this chapter about how their actions can affect their reputation.
- If your child is open to it, try role-playing in which you are the peer trying to convince your child to do something counterproductive, then switch roles and model how your child can choose a healthier path without necessarily losing a friendship.
- These days, social media is a key way kids communicate. Periodically remind your child of the dangers of cyberbullying, the

permanence of most texts and posts, and how even colleges have been known to check on the "technological imprint" of potential students.

- During a conversation ask, "Do you really want that photo to go viral? You may be sending it to a friend, but you don't know who else might see it or receive it." Both verbal posts and pictures can affect your child's reputation, and this is a discussion worth having in different forms over time as your child becomes more comfortable with his posts and may develop a false sense of privacy while sending texts, pictures, tweets, and so forth.

The goal of these conversations is not to be critical of your child, but to help your child understand the ramifications of sending messages and learn to self-monitor according to the information you have shared.

For rebellious children, you might add a few other comments. In a moment when there is no tension, you can commend your child on wanting to "change the world," "think for himself," and be "confident in his decisions." Simultaneously, though, talk about how you are not the enemy; you are a sounding board and want to help your child learn to self-monitor so that he continues to feel confident in making healthy decisions.

As you know, children and teenagers have a way of shutting out adults if they believe they are being criticized or their opinions or feelings are being discounted. Of course, there are times when parents have to be the judge and not support their child's decision. This can often be reserved for when your child is about to do something dangerous or irreversible (e.g., joining friends to throw snowballs at passing cars, riding in the car with a driver who had been drinking).

If your child complains that you are causing her to lose friends because of your family rules, you may wonder how good these friends really are for your child. Stating this may only lead to your child's taking on a defensive stance. However, using key examples may give your child something to think about. Carla's mother, for example, reminded her daughter of the incident when her two friends, Cindy and Hayley, made fun of her because she wouldn't use the cheat sheet they created for a test. They put pressure on her to not be "such a baby and good girl." Carla, remembering this and other incidents, decided she was more comfortable following the family rules than forcing herself to fit in when it made her feel bad about herself and her choices. Because both of Carla's parents were supportive of her and proud of her for her ability to make sound and independent decisions, it was easier for Carla to seek out a peer group that accepted her for being herself.

There are some children who lack confidence and have few friends. These children may have anxiety, or may even panic, over the thought that they may act in a way that causes them to lose the few friends they have. The dilemma occurs when your child wants to self-monitor and make decisions she would normally feel pride in making, but these same actions might simultaneously lead to her friends rejecting her. In this case, you may want to consult a professional on how to help your child be "true to herself" and not compromise healthy values because of a strong need to belong and gain peer acceptance.

At times, seeking a professional to guide you is essential and is often quite useful. However, don't overlook the fact that you may have some helpful friends, relatives, and community members who will also be able to share some good ideas for guiding your child when it comes to peer acceptance and self-monitoring, as well as a variety of other topics.

For instance, 12-year-old Brandon loved acting; he was in his school plays and focused all his energy on singing, acting, and dancing. He put far less energy into his academic work. Brandon frequently told his parents he was going to be an actor and didn't have to get good grades for college. One day, the family was visiting his grandmother in a senior center when this topic came up once again. Brandon's grandmother suggested he talk to the former actress who was sitting at the next table. Brandon loved the idea of talking to someone who shared his interests. However, 20 minutes later, he had learned more than he had expected. Brandon learned that being an actor often does not pay the bills and he needed a backup plan. Hearing this advice from someone who also loved the theater left a big impression on him, and he began to care more about studying, although he didn't decrease his focus on the arts. Brandon learned how to balance his avocation with his daily responsibilities. You can find helpful people in the most unlikely places.

Talk With Your Child About Moderation

Children may not always know the meaning of the phrase "too much of a good thing." A child who likes dolls may want as many as possible but may run out of money to buy them and space to house them. A child who loves eating chocolate may attempt to eat an entire chocolate cake and end up with an upset stomach. The teenager who does not understand moderation may choose to socialize at the expense of balancing social time with studying.

Teaching moderation may not make you popular. But it can help your child have a successful life. Toddlers can begin to understand the basic concept of moderation even though, emotionally, it's often difficult for them to accept. As children get older, they are often more capable of understanding this concept of moderation, whether it's about how they spend their time, what they do with their money, or what they focus on learning.

Ryan, for example, at the age of 4 wanted to spend all his waking hours watching cartoons. He didn't care whether he watched them on the computer, iPad, or television, but he was insistent on watching them. He preferred to eat his meals while watching the cartoons and even refused to go to bed when he was exhausted because he wanted to make sure he saw the full hour of cartoons at night. There were many nights when Ryan fell asleep with the iPad in his hands.

Ryan's parents were concerned about his excessive focus on these cartoons. They sought the guidance of a child psychologist, Dr. Golden. Dr. Golden explained that many children of Ryan's age struggle with moderation but that it's an essential lesson for them to learn so that they can have varied life experiences and increase their ability to adapt to many situations. Ryan's parents limited his viewing of cartoons, and Ryan responded by having loud, long tantrums.

To avoid his tantrums, Ryan's parents initially wanted to give in to his demand to watch cartoons. However, they implemented several recommendations from the psychologist. The following is the plan of action that eventually led Ryan to become more flexible and better able to tolerate moderation, including having some of his cartoon watching being limited.

- Ryan's parents informed him that all electronics would only be used in the household at specific times (which were clearly explained).
- Ryan was given a number of fun options with which to fill his time because he did not know, on his own, what to do with his extra time.
- Ryan's parents kept him busy with activities outside the home, where he was distracted, had more time to have social interactions, and was entertained in many different ways.
- Despite his tantrums, Ryan's parents kept to their new rules and refused to give in to his insistence c~ ~ ~ ~ for longer periods. They did not yell at (stop the tantrums because this often esca

- Dr. Golden suggested that when Ryan had tantrums, his parents should make sure Ryan was safe, but realize tantrum time is not a time for discussion. Ryan's parents were instructed to calmly state, "When you're done with your tantrum, we can talk."

At first, Ryan's tantrums lasted for long periods, and he was resistant to alternative activities. Within a relatively short time frame, however, Ryan's parents noticed signs that he was enjoying some other activities and beginning to accept the fact that cartoons could only be watched in moderation.

Throughout the growing years, the lesson of learning moderation is important. Elementary school children can sometimes find an activity they love and want to spend most of their day doing. Anna wanted to do origami rather than study or even pay attention in class. Eric wanted to play basketball all day, and when not playing because he was sitting in class, he tried to spend his time studying the stats of professional players by looking at sports magazines.

Anna may grow up to be an accomplished artist, and Eric may end up in the NBA. Encouraging some focus on their interests can be productive. Focusing at the expense of learning other skills can be counterproductive. Anna's parents eventually said to her,

> It's great to be an artist, but it's difficult to be so famous that you can support yourself. Along with studying art, and doing your origami, it would be a good idea to learn other skills so you have more careers to choose from when you are older. You may end up picking a career that includes being creative, such as architecture or commercial art.

The following actions on your part can benefit elementary school children who are learning how to accept moderation.

- Acknowledge that you understand that they are passionate about their area of interest and work hard at it.
- Ask them to share their feelings, including pleasurable ones, about activities they engaged in during the day (e.g., schoolwork, chores, family outings, sometimes engaging in games that are more interesting to a friend than to them).
- Ask them to pick one activity they did in the last day, week, or month that they would be willing to focus on more and develop more skills for (e.g., ice skating, singing, learning a foreign language).
- Seek their input into how they can continue to focus on their passions, yet meet obligations.
- Sometimes a behavior modification program can help some children (e.g., getting points for engaging in alternative activities, and once they reach a certain number of points, they get a mutually agreed-on reward to acknowledge their efforts).
- If you find your child has given up his strong interest entirely, encourage him to return to it but not exclusively.

These strategies and some of the strategies Ryan's parents used when he was a preschool child also worked years later when he was a tween. The words parents use may get more sophisticated, but the basic concepts can generally help growing children through the years.

Moderation does not mean abandoning one's interest or preferences. It simply means engaging in them to a lesser degree and adding more areas of focus. One example of moderation that often makes sense to elementary school-aged children is to explain, "Too much water is not good. It leads to floods. Too little water is also not good. It leads to drought. Too much focus on one activity leads to depriving yourself of learning other activities."

In the teenage years, not practicing moderation can lead to some destructive activities. Sometimes an adolescent becomes "obsessed" with a crush and abandons all other interests because of a perceived need to be constantly around that person. Other teenagers may feel the need to constantly "party" or even constantly study. However, not focusing on peers, dating, and schoolwork can lead to isolation, loneliness, or academic neglect.

Teenagers who have previously learned how to communicate in a dialogue rather than monologue have established executive functioning skills, have learned to tolerate frustration, and can recognize the potential consequences of their behaviors are more likely to find a balance in the adolescent years.

When teenagers lack moderation, they may be so focused on themselves and their own preferences that they tune out the advice of others. This "tuning out" may take the form of rebellion and dismissing even sound and logical guidance. If the tuning out and focusing on their thoughts and desires leads the teenager to be unproductive or engaged in destructive excesses, it may be time to consult with a mental health professional to help you help your teenager find a way to avoid these behaviors.

The Always-Present Power of the Parent

As a child, did you ever act differently when your parents were around versus when they were not around? It is not unusual for children and teenagers to act differently when an adult is present as opposed to when there is no adult around.

Many parents have been upset when they learn of their child's actions when they were not there to supervise. Have you (or your own parents) ever said, "What were you thinking? How could you have acted that way?" These are good questions to ask your child if the tone and the wording are not conveyed in an overly critical fashion and part of your goal in asking is to encourage self-reflection and self-evaluation.

The difference in behavior that children can display when no adult is present can occur for a number of reasons.

- Impulsivity, or acting before thinking, can often be an issue for toddlers and for impulsive older children who benefit from the structure of an adult's supervision. Note that impulsivity is not the same as a child not caring about her reputation or what she did when she was calm enough to reflect. In fact, these children may struggle with their self-esteem when they feel that they, once again, disappointed themselves or an adult about whom they care.
- Some children have not been coached in decision making, so when no adult is present to guide them, they flounder.
- Many parents assume that children who do not act in the way they were taught to behave must be rebelling. Certainly, there are children and even more teenagers who do rebel, but this does not necessarily have to be the case.
- Another adult might tell you that in your absence, your child has been acting in ways that can be dangerous (e.g., riding a bicycle without heeding the directive to wear a helmet). Try discussing this report with your child, without accusation but with concern. You may learn more about what is happening with your child, and your child will hopefully be open to listening to you!

Did you know that some children act more appropriately when they are not around parents or other guiding adults? When this happens, it is often a time when parents realize their children have absorbed what was taught over the years and are becoming more capable of applying their knowledge to everyday situations and growing into independent individuals! At home, they may relinquish the monitoring of their behavior to you, despite having the skills that they show when you are not around. This is not all that uncommon for young children.

Sometimes your child acts differently when you are not present, not because he disagrees with or disrespects your rules but because he believes he can make some different but equally good decisions on how to act in his social, athletic, or academic worlds. For instance, Seth, age 10, thought that his mother was too nervous about kids getting hurt while playing football. She had told Seth he should never play that sport. When Seth was hanging out with a group of his friends, he remembered his mother's wishes but felt that because she had never played the game, he knew better, and he knew how to play and minimize the chances he would get injured. As long as his mother was not around, Seth joined his friends when they started a football game. Luckily, Seth did not get hurt, but his mother picked him up early from his friend's home one day and saw that her son was playing football.

Seth's mother felt angry that he had defied her, anxious that he could get injured in the future, and hurt that Seth did not take her concerns seriously. Seth's father, after hearing his wife's reaction, said, "Children have to take risks sometimes. If you say he can play, maybe a compromise can be figured out." Seth and his parents eventually were able to have a calm discussion, during which Seth explained that he does not play tackle but rather flag football with no tackling and no blocking. Seth's mother admitted she had over-reacted without even having all the information and that he had, in fact, used good judgment.

Unfortunately, not all children make the best decisions when no adult is there to supervise. Charlotte, for instance, was a physically mature 13-year-old. She began hanging around with older girls and believed that getting their approval was more important than pleasing her parents. She began drinking beer and hanging out with boys. When she heard she was getting a bad reputation at school, she came home crying to her mother. Charlotte acknowledged she had made choices that she would never have made if her mother were chaperoning the parties. She regretted having made the choices she did.

For Charlotte, the desire to gain the approval of these older friends led her to ignore her ability to consider consequences of her actions before things got a bit out of hand. Charlotte hugged her mother and said, "Mom, I thought you were just old and nagging. I should have listened to you. You are actually pretty smart." Charlotte's mother was considering getting professional help for Charlotte because of the seriousness of her behavior, but Charlotte's response made it unnecessary at that time, as long as she continued on the path of insight and change.

Seth and Charlotte, as well as many other children, have the ability to have an internal dialogue with their parents when their parents are not present. Kids generally know what their parent would approve of, disapprove of, be proud of, and be concerned about.

It might be helpful to let your child know you truly are always there, even if it's just your words resonating in the back of her mind if she takes the time to listen. You can even make it a game over dinner. Referring to a particular situation that was described on television or occurred that day, ask your child whether she wants to guess what your response might be. You might be surprised at how well she knows your reactions.

Kids Watch You, So Model What You Want Them to See!

Have you heard the phrase "Do as I say, not as I do"? Many parents throughout the generations have said this. Sometimes it is simply an admission that the parent isn't perfect and doesn't want the child to copy mistakes. At other times, parents give themselves permission to act in ways they would not approve of in their children. Either way, children often learn more from watching than from listening to the advice of grown-ups. The well-known psychologist Jean Piaget frequently highlighted the benefit of children modeling from others as they develop their moral standards.

Through modeling, children not only learn about how to act in the community but also how to manage responsibilities, how to think before reacting, how to look at the glass as half empty or half full, and so forth. For example, Aaron, at the age of 10, frequently noticed that his father displayed "road rage," even when another driver simply entered his lane and ended up close to his car. Aaron was often tense in the car with his father, yet Aaron later displayed similar signs of temper when there were minor disagreements on the playground at school. When Aaron's mother questioned him after she received a call from his teacher about his behavior, Aaron said, "You need to show people they can't mess with you! I learned that from dad!" After Aaron's parents had spoken privately about his comments, his father sat down with Aaron and apologized for teaching Aaron a lesson that was detrimental for him to model.

Children model the behavior of parents in many other areas as well. You probably already realize that when a child is told to "spend wisely," a child will often think, "Getting what I want is wise!" They may not be weighing short-term versus long-term goals or need versus want. In addition, when a parent spends frivolously, their child is more likely to learn that it is okay to spend this way, despite the cautious admonition to "spend wisely."

Danielle, at the age of 11, often went clothes shopping with her mother. She noticed her mother limited the amount she spent on most items, set a cap on her spending for the day, and thought twice about getting something on sale if it wasn't really a discount price or she really didn't need it. In fact, Danielle's mother and Danielle often played the "Can I Beat That Price?" game. They used an app on the phone to check the prices of comparable items in other locations.

When shopping, Danielle's mother said aloud, seemingly to herself but really for Danielle to hear, "Do I really need this, or do I just really want this? If I just want it, can I afford to splurge today?" At the age of 13, Danielle and her friend Kira were shopping for clothes in one part of the store while her father looked for items in another department. Danielle had fun trying on lots of clothing, but she put most items back on the rack and said, "I don't really need this, and don't love it enough to spend money on it rather than splurge on something else." Kira teased Danielle about being "so cheap" as she took many items to the cashier to buy with her birthday money.

Two months after the shopping spree, Danielle told Kira she was excited because she had just got home from shopping with her mother and had bought herself the laptop she had wanted for months. Kira admitted to being jealous and asked, "How did you afford it? I never seem to have any money." Danielle reminded Kira, in a friendly manner, that Kira had called Danielle "so cheap" earlier that year. Danielle taught her friend the money-spending lesson she had learned from observing her mother's spending habits.

Whether they are positive or negative lessons, kids watch and learn from those adults whom they admire and love. The following are some tips on how to help your child learn through your modeling:

- If you make a mistake, don't ignore it. Explain how you would do things differently if you had an opportunity to go back in time. Explain how you can change things now, if you have the opportunity, and how you would do things differently if a similar situation arises in the future.
- If you make a positive choice, you may later want to point out the options you had and why you ended up making the choice you did.

- Model that you can change your mind if new information warrants it; this is modeling flexible and adaptive thinking.
- Apologize if you are wrong so that your child learns there is no shame in apologizing.

It can be exhausting to realize that children are watching and learning from you and other adults whom they look up to all day long. However, it's a compliment to you when they mimic your actions and your decisions. If you are helping your child to be an independent thinker, there will be times she will try to use her problem-solving skills and forget to model yours. This is just a time for discussion and learning.

Learning From Mistakes So As Not to Repeat Them

Some children become defensive and deny their mistakes because they are uncomfortable, afraid of punishment, worried about risking upsetting their parents, or even simply embarrassed about their actions when caught. Children who are open to learning from mistakes are children who truly trust grown-ups to help rather than judge and who have a healthy level of confidence that they are okay despite their mistake.

All parents have children who make mistakes. In fact, anyone who explores new skills or experiences is likely to make some mistakes. At different ages, children encounter new social, athletic, academic, and societal situations. A child may make a mistake because of inexperience, a lack of decision-making skills or coping strategies, impulsivity, or a host of other reasons. Parents who listen to their child's explanation are parents who have the opportunity to learn more about their child and get a better idea of how to help their child correct his behavior in the future.

The following are some ways to foster open and nonjudgmental communication after learning that your child made a mistake (whether it was because of a purposeful action or accidental):

- Your third-grade son, for instance, decided to invite all the boys in his class to a party except one boy whom he didn't like. He later regretted his decision when he learned that this boy was crying over the perceived rejection. Listening to your son's rationale for his omission and his feelings now are a great way to open communication.
- Ask questions, but be aware that your tone of voice can convey different messages. Make sure to have discussions face-to-face, and try asking clear questions such as, "What did you want to happen?" "Can you fill me in from your point of view about what happened?"
- Before responding to your child, take a moment to remember that you probably made mistakes when you were young and that learning from them helped shape you into a successful adult.
- Share some appropriate examples of mistakes you have made and how you corrected them, so your child knows that even grown-ups can learn from mistakes.
- Together, try to find the lesson in the situation and how your child could learn not to repeat the mistake in the future.

A child who periodically makes mistakes is often a child who is exploring and trying to learn how to navigate through new experiences. It's a time to guide her, so you should not be too concerned when this occurs. However, if your child consistently makes and repeats mistakes without learning from the prior incidents, it can be problematic.

There are numerous reasons why children repeat mistakes: they are impulsive and not considering consequences, they feel a strong need to repeat the behavior, they want to prove they were right all along that the behavior was not a mistake, and so forth. If your child consistently makes mistakes and does not respond to your guidance, you may want to seek the advice of a mental health professional about the best way to help your child avoid the repetition of mistakes.

BEWARE OF THE LESSON OF THE "WOODEN SPOON"

Trying to teach children lessons through intimidation can teach many unwanted lessons. Parents may spend a lot of time and energy yelling, threatening consequences, and even trying physical punishment (it is always best to avoid this!) as a way to get through to their children and guide them onto a productive path. Despite their efforts, parents are often left with children who do not confide in them, who hide information to avoid punishments, and who even resent their parents.

Paul's father felt it was unnatural to remain calm and talk to his son about "his lack of judgment." Instead, he yelled at Paul and frequently scolded him for his transgressions. Paul learned not to confide in his father, and Paul's father felt exhausted that his son didn't listen to his loud advice. Even though Paul sometimes agreed with his father's views about the potential risk to his reputation if he continued certain behaviors, he never shared this with his father because of his anger at how his father was treating him. In fact, he continued certain behaviors out of rebellion rather than because he thought it was the best option.

As you probably already know, to have open communication with children they have to feel they can trust and confide in you. If you disapprove of certain actions, try to find a way to make it clear to your child that you don't disapprove of her, but you only disapprove of her actions. When parents discuss rather than yell, children are able to absorb the messages and then use them to monitor and adjust their behavior, rather than rebelling, when their parents are not there.

TEACHING YOUR CHILD TO ACCEPT SELF-CONSEQUENCES

Taking healthy risks is an important part of any child's growth. It allows them to develop self-confidence for being able to try new things and even to handle making some mistakes in the process. When children are afraid that mistakes are not correctable and reflect on their lack of competence, they may hesitate to take on new experiences.

Children who are overly critical of their errors often end up administering harsh self-consequences, such as calling themselves names (e.g., "I'm such an idiot") and promising never to attempt that challenge again. Children who learn when it's healthy to take on new risks and that many mistakes can be corrected are less likely to judge themselves too negatively. In addition, when they understand the appropriate ways to respond when they make choices that are not appropriate for themselves, others, or the situation, these children are often more likely to administer healthy self-consequences involving self-reflection and restitution when appropriate (e.g., "I'll never do that again. I really regret doing that. I'm going to apologize to my friend for making that joke and embarrassing her" or "I'll never do that again. What was I thinking? It scared me and was not the brightest thing I ever did!"). Self-consequences ca~ ᵎ ful when they serve as reminders to your child th~ repeat the mistake and can also lead h~ decide to repair any damage th~

Self-consequences are what consequences you, as ᵎ thoughts you share about ho and then by having the opportu independently. There are certaiᵎ make some decisions on their own that are not dangerous and can be reversed, allowing them to brainstorm appropriate consequences when needed for their actions.

If, for instance, you are at home and your 4-year-old child is beginning to pour some milk, and a small amount drips onto the table, you can overlook it and use the experience to start a discussion about whether she is ready to do this again, could benefit from some techniques for how to pour milk, or still needs help. However, if a child of any age wants to stick things in a light socket, it is obviously not the time to allow this behavior in the hopes of your child learning the consequences of this action!

One thing that is almost guaranteed is that life will not always be easy or pleasant and injustices may even occur. Each time your child experiences the stress of an injustice, you can seize the moment as a learning opportunity. Sometimes, in an attempt to protect their child and correct the injustice, parents support their youngster without focusing on how to develop coping strategies (for now and for the future) when presented with this and similar difficult situations. However, sometimes a child or teenager feels there has been an injustice when it's just a disappointing or stressful situation.

Mr. Levitt was a social studies teacher in a suburban high school. Peter, a student in his AP (advanced placement) World History class, was consistently disrupting the class, making jokes about various cultural traditions, failing to hand in homework, and frequently cutting class. Mr. Levitt gave Peter a D for the semester.

Mr. Levitt was then called into the principal's office, where he met with the principal and Peter's mother. Peter's mother expressed rage that her son received such a low grade. Mr. Levitt responded saying,

frequently failed to hand in his homework, did not appropriately join in class discussions, and got low test grades. I tried to reach out to your son on many occasions to talk about how he was doing, but Peter never showed up for the scheduled appointments. I left several messages for you as well, but unfortunately, I never received a return call.

The principal explained to Peter's mother,

We know Peter has historically been a fine student. That's how he got into the AP class. However, it's not acceptable to give him a grade that he didn't earn. I do understand, though, that his grade can hurt him when he applies to college.

The principal then turned to Mr. Levitt and asked whether he had any suggestions on how to help Peter. Despite the pressure from Peter's mother, Mr. Levitt did not offer to change Peter's grade. He did offer some hope, however. Mr. Levitt said, "If Peter is more productive and responsible in the upcoming semester, he could certainly raise his grade."

Peter's mother insisted that her son's performance was not typical of him and must be due to some shortcoming of Mr. Levitt, who had failed to engage and motivate her son. She left the meeting abruptly, believing that this problem was due to the teacher's incompetence. Rather than learning the need to self-monitor and use executive functioning skills, Peter learned a very different lesson. His mother informed him, "It's not your fault that you got a D. Mr. Levitt doesn't know how to motivate kids and teach so you can easily learn. Let's get you out of his class, so the grade doesn't show up on your college transcript." Peter happily dropped out of the ˌ ˌˌontinued to blame his teacher for his poor performance.

If Peter was your son, how would you ᴴ ation? Do you think his mother's protection capped him for his future academic and empl Peter's parents had the opportunity to hav son about his role in getting his grade and ways to avoid such situations in the future (e.g., becoming more organized, accepting help when needed, going to class on time, completing homework). Peter might not have been as happy if he had to accept this accountability, but he would have had a better chance to correct his actions and would have been better prepared for similar situations in the future.

SUMMARY

In this chapter, you read about key ways parents can help their children learn to monitor their behavior. In addition, some ways to keep the lines of communication open with children, even when discussing their errors of judgment or mistakes, were reviewed. In the upcoming chapter, ways to foster social competence are explored.

CHAPTER 7

SOCIAL SKILLS: BUILDING YOUR CHILD'S SOCIAL COMPETENCE

Most infants smile at people and enjoy a game of peek-a-boo. Social interactions and skills are simply a natural part of normal development. As children get a bit older, however, parents often realize that turn taking, matching behaviors to the appropriate time and place, reading another person's body language, and making and keeping friendships are things that can be more complicated.

In this chapter, you will read about how to prepare your child to interact in the social world around him, relate with others, interpret words and verbal intonations of others, read body language, and deal with rejection and even bullying. In addition, you will read about how you can prepare your child to maximize his ability to socially interact in a manner that can open doors and allow him to reach more goals.

Before reading further, take a minute to reflect on how you foster the development of social skills and competence in your child.

For each item listed below, fill in the number that corresponds best to your response:

(continues)

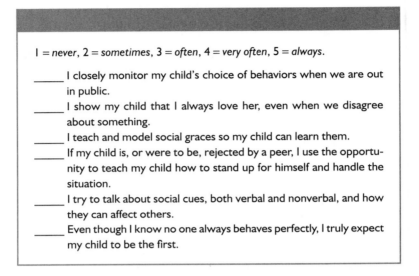

1 = *never*, 2 = *sometimes*, 3 = *often*, 4 = *very often*, 5 = *always*.

_____ I closely monitor my child's choice of behaviors when we are out in public.

_____ I show my child that I always love her, even when we disagree about something.

_____ I teach and model social graces so my child can learn them.

_____ If my child is, or were to be, rejected by a peer, I use the opportunity to teach my child how to stand up for himself and handle the situation.

_____ I try to talk about social cues, both verbal and nonverbal, and how they can affect others.

_____ Even though I know no one always behaves perfectly, I truly expect my child to be the first.

There are many children and adults who feel that social success is about controlling a situation and others. A leader who is more like a dictator is viewed very differently than a leader who motivates the group to work toward a common goal. A child who feels capable of matching his behavior to the right situation, knows how to connect respectfully with adults as well as with peers, and has the ability to collaborate with others is a child who is well on his way toward social competence. This chapter offers some tips for helping your child move forward on the road toward this social competence.

THE ART OF COMMUNICATION

Effective communication is an integral part of social competence. The art of communication means knowing more than how to listen and speak. When speaking, it's helpful to consider time, place, person, and context. For instance, if your child starts a serious discussion just before his school bus arrives, and it's not urgent, you should acknowledge the importance of his statement and suggest that discussing it after school would give both of you the time you need to talk about it.

The setting or *place* is also important to consider when deciding how and when to communicate. Imagine if your child started telling jokes with friends in a quiet movie theater. Now, imagine if your child were at home with friends and telling the same jokes. Even if the jokes were age appropriate, one setting would breed negative reactions from others, whereas the latter setting would be the right one for those interactions.

The next point to consider is *person*. Imagine how a teacher would feel if a student unexpectedly referred to her by her first name when this was not the accepted way for students to address teachers in that school. If a student is speaking with a teacher, the style of communication is often different than it is when interacting with a peer. Some children need more guidance than others on how to match their actions and words with the time, setting, and the person with whom they are talking.

To learn about context, it's fun to try to describe a comment and have the rest of the family guess (from multiple choice options) the meaning behind it. For instance, you overhear one child say to a classmate, "You were strike happy yesterday." Without knowing whether they were talking about bowling or baseball, it's hard to know the true intention behind the comment. "Strike happy" in bowling would be great! In baseball, not so much. By talking about the possible multiple meanings or interpretations of comments, your child will develop a better ability to ask clarifying questions. This is especially important for situations in which there's no body language or tone of voice to interpret, as with texting and social media.

A SIMPLE THANK YOU IS NICE!

Simple statements such as "hi," "thank you," or "please" are all social graces that even toddlers can learn to use at appropriate times.

Scott's parents understood that being polite can lead to positive feedback from others. Even before Scott was able to talk, his parents always modeled the use of these quick phrases, such as by saying, "Hi, Scott!" or "Thank you for this beautiful drawing!" When Scott was a toddler, he began to imitate some of his parents' expressions. At the age of 2, sitting in his highchair at a restaurant, Scott said, "Thank you!" to the waiter when his food was delivered. The waiter did a double take then left the table smiling. It is never too early to start modeling these social graces for your child.

Have you ever held the door open for someone who walked through but never even gave you a simple "thank you"? If so, how did that make you feel? Many of us, in a moment of self-reflection, can admit to at least one time when we were so focused on something that we were too distracted to use our social graces. Children may also have social graces but be distracted and not use them. However, some children may not be distracted but do not show social graces because they simply don't know what to do and when to do it.

Jamie, for example, was excited to go to her sixth-grade dance at school. At the dance, she was standing with three of her girlfriends when Lance, a boy from her class whom she liked, came over to talk. After talking about the event for a few minutes, Lance asked Jamie whether she wanted to dance. Jamie hated dancing but wanted to talk to and hang out with Lance. She looked him in the eyes and said, "I don't want to." Lance, thinking that Jamie didn't like him, walked away and eventually started dancing with another girl. Jamie was hurt and didn't know what she had done, or hadn't done, to make him walk away. Her friend, at Jamie's insistence, went over to Lance the next school day and asked what had happened. He said, "She didn't like me, so I moved on." When her friend contradicted his perception, he said, "She didn't smile. She didn't thank me for asking. She didn't say she wanted to hang out but just not dance. How was I supposed to know?" Jamie had not learned the clear communication and social skills that matched the setting of being at a dance.

For children, each new experience brings new opportunities to learn social graces (e.g., the power of a smile or a simple "please"). Although there are etiquette classes that teach social competence, you have the power to teach, explain, and model these skills on a daily basis. Of course, no matter how much adults say "Do as I say, not as I do," children will likely do as you do, not as you say. This may put a bit of pressure on you, but try to remember that preparing your child for independence is certainly a worthwhile goal.

The following are some tips for helping your child develop polite, respectful, and caring social communication behaviors.

- As always, being a role model highlights that you value these actions when interacting with your child as well as with others.
- Use socially polite words (e.g., "thank you") when talking with others.
- Use socially polite actions (e.g., holding the door open for others, giving up your seat on a train to a more needy person).
- Politely correct your child when she forgets or did not know a situation called for social graces.
- If a person is not polite to your family, use it as an opportunity to talk with your child about how the other person could have handled things in a more appropriate way.

Children tend to use social graces more naturally and more willingly if they understand that doing so is not just a habit but has an important impact on themselves and on others. A person who uses socially polite words and actions is generally a person who has a positive reputation. In fact, having a positive reputation can affect children when they interact with peers, teachers, family members, and later, with bosses. Therefore, it is truly an essential skill to learn.

In addition, as you know, using social graces can show others that you are considerate of their feelings, care about being respectful, and care about the needs of others. Therefore, social graces are more than a quick "please" or "thank you."

Part of social graces is doing, but another part is omitting. Imagine if Zachary, age 10, always held the door open for others and often used polite words such as "please" or "thank you." However, at lacrosse practice, he heard a few of his friends repeatedly using racial slurs, and Zachary wanted to fit in. Therefore, he sometimes used them at lacrosse practice or at school even though he knew these comments were not appropriate.

Zachary was initially confused when a few of his school friends were no longer available for get-togethers and hung out with others at lunch instead. Zachary felt he was a loyal friend and was hurt by these reactions. He talked to his parents about it but said he honestly did not know why these friendships had changed. He gave his parents permission to talk with the parents of one of his friends.

Zachary's parents were in disbelief at what the other parent reported about Zachary. They sat down with Zachary and said,

> Richard's parents said he was offended by some racial insults you have been saying. He's embarrassed to be around you now because of this. You know we don't use those kinds of words in our family. They can be highly offensive.

Zachary immediately began to cry and admitted he didn't like using the words but was trying to fit in. When asked about what lesson he learned from this experience, Zachary said, "I should just be me, try to care about everyone, and not try to act differently just to fit in. If I have to act different, maybe those aren't my real friends."

Feel free to share Zachary's story with your child. Situations will arise in your family that are good teaching moments as well. In fact, even watching television shows together can be used as casual lessons about what helps and does not help others to respect someone and the need to show respect to others. In Chapter 8, the social graces in social media are explored.

VERBAL INTONATIONS: HOW YOU SAY IT CAN CHANGE ITS MEANING

Children may not realize that a handwritten or typed letter, an e-mail, or a text may not convey the subtle nuances that explain the intent behind the spoken word. For instance, the following statements can communicate very different meanings, depending on one's tone of voice.

- "Yeah, right!" The sincere intent: The statement communicates support for what another person shared. The sarcastic intent: The statement communicates disbelief and/or disapproval of the statement of another person.
- "That's good enough?" versus "That's good enough." The sincere intent (communicating a period at the end of the sentence): The statement reflects a belief that the performance met certain criteria. The sarcastic intent (communicating a question mark at the end of the sentence): The statement reflects a disbelief that minimum standards were met.

Sometimes friends get upset with each other when they misread the other's voice inflections. Imagine how hard it is to understand the intent when you don't hear the other's words because you are reading them.

You are probably aware of some of the typical messages voice intonations convey. Of course, body language (which is addressed in the upcoming section) communicates a lot as well, often overlapping with the verbal message. The challenge of communicating over technology, when voice inflections and body language are not seen, is explored in Chapter 8.

You can share with your child the meaning of voice intonations:

- Boredom or not being interested in what your child is saying is conveyed if the listener responds minimally, keeps saying "Huh?" or "Yeah" or "What?" or "Whatever," and has a flat tone of voice.
- Interest in—not boredom with—what your child is saying can be conveyed when the listener engages in a dialogue, adds to the discussion, or has a more energized tone of voice.
- Impatience, annoyance, or lack of interest is conveyed through curt responses (e.g., one-word sentences or comments such as "Whatever," "Right," "Sure"); however, sometimes a one-word sentence (e.g., "Right" or "Sure") simply communicates agreement—tone of voice may help your child determine the meaning behind the word.
- Speaking characteristics can communicate more than the words alone can (e.g., speaking rapidly when impatient, restating another's comments to show active listening, showing caring through tone of voice, raising the voice at the end of a sentence to communicate a question or exclamation).
- Volume of voice can give additional cues about what the speaker is communicating (e.g., simply matching volume to the setting, such as whispering in a library, shows respect for surroundings; whispering may also convey that a conversation is private or secret; a loud voice may communicate strong emotion or passion; a loud voice may also show enthusiasm at a sporting event; typical volume conveys a conversational tone).

In addition to voice inflections, some words confuse children because they take them literally rather than realizing they are being used as an idiom, metaphor, or simile. Adults have learned the importance of voice intonation and these other means of expression, but for children, and those for whom English is a second language, learning these tools can be key to becoming better communicators.

The following are some ways to teach your child about voice inflections, the appropriate use of idioms, and being an effective verbal communicator:

- If you believe according to her voice intonation that your child sounds bored, angry, or impatient, ask whether this is accurate and discuss the miscommunication if it is not.
- Games can be fun. Over dinner or in the car, see whether each person can make the same statement with a different meaning (e.g., "Oh, yeah, Uncle Joe is coming to dinner").
- If you realize you are using a tone of voice that is different than usual, clarify your intent (e.g., you are exhausted, not exasperated).
- Children may express impatience and anger to you when describing a frustrating situation. Help your child use the tone for the event, not for your interaction (i.e., expressing feelings to you, not at you).

BODY LANGUAGE AND APPEARANCES SPEAK VOLUMES

Do you remember your reaction when you saw the first smile on your child's face? At that moment, many parents are filled with love, excitement, and a feeling that their child is happy and connected to them. If this happened to you, you know the power of body language!

Children sometimes spontaneously use body language, such as making a pouting face when upset, having a visible temper tantrum when frustrated, or smiling and even jumping up and dov when excited. However, they do not always think about how their behavior and nonverbal communication affect others, and they do not always pay attention to the body language of others.

Facial Expressions

The many muscles in the face show a wide variety of emotions. However, sometimes one look represents different expressions of feelings and has different meanings for different people. For example, Frank's children often thought he was angry when he came home from work, but he was just simply exhausted. Frank had to use words to explain his facial expressions to his children.

Raised eyebrows can express surprise, fear, or a judgmental or arrogant attitude. Whoever said that reading facial expressions is easy? Children lack experience narrowing down the true meaning of facial expressions and may not be able to understand how the combination of the expression with other body language and verbal cues conveys what a person is trying to share.

There are many ways to help your child understand this form of communication.

- Make a game out of it. Write many different emotion words on pieces of paper and have each family member pick one. Have them show that emotion only by using facial expressions while others try to guess it.
- Sometimes ask your child to guess what you are feeling according to your facial expression. If she is inaccurate, add words and verbal intonations. If she gets it then, it's a good lesson on how facial expressions and words combine to increase effective communication.
- If your young child is making a facial expression (e.g., happy, mad, sad), comment on it and see whether you were right,

highlighting for your child that he or she also communicates with facial expressions.

- Offer respectful questions your child can ask to clarify whether she is accurately interpreting someone's facial expressions (e.g., "You look like you are mad at me. Are you?" or "I know you got into the spelling bee, but you don't look happy. What's up?").

The look on one's face can communicate a lot, but sometimes it leads to miscommunication. If your child learns how to read facial expressions and knows how to check whether his interpretations are right (rather than assuming they are), he will be better able to understand others.

Other Physical Expressions

Imagine you are standing next to your child talking while you have your arms folded. Now, add a smile and complimentary words. Your child may not think the folded arms are a sign of disapproval. However, if you just call her name and stand with folded arms, she may focus more on the body language and feel she has done something wrong in your eyes.

Children are often comfortable running, jumping, and playing. However, they may not pay too much attention to how close they stand to another person or how that affects that person. Many adults have had the discomfort of riding a train or bus when a stranger has encroached on their personal space. To help your child avoid becoming this person, teaching about socially appropriate proximity to others is an important lesson.

The tricky part about teaching appropriate distance between your child and others is that it can vary. Standing close to, or even hugging, a parent is appropriate at most, if not all, ages. However, when an 11-year-old stands too close to peers, it can create discomfort or even a feeling of intimidation on the part of the other children, especially ones who are not that child's best friends. In addition, standing too close to a teacher may be seen as inappropriate even though the child may simply be communicating a need for support or comfort.

There are other lessons to teach about body expressions. How your child stands can communicate a lot. For instance, Kelly had a habit of standing with one foot forward and tapping the toes of that foot against the floor. One day, when her teacher spoke with her about her test grade, Kelly stood in this manner. Her teacher felt that she was communicating an "I-don't-care" attitude. Kelly was embarrassed and confused when her teacher commented on this.

How people stand and what they do with their arms (when speaking and also when listening) can let another person know whether they are engaged in the discussion, bored, angry, pleased, and so forth. Some body language is clear. If you are talking with your child and he rolls his eyes, you can make a fairly good guess that you are not getting through to him. However, many people have had their body language misinterpreted.

To help your child be aware of the messages given through body language, you could use the following tips:

- Expand the game you played with facial expressions to include more nonverbal communication.
- While watching a TV show, turn off the volume and see whether you and your child can guess what is happening by watching the body language of the actors.
- If your child stands in certain ways, ask her (in a nonaccusatory way) whether your interpretation of her feelings is accurate.
- If you catch yourself using body language that doesn't match your intended message, comment aloud about it and change your body language.

Your child may appreciate the power of body language if you use the example of what a single finger can indicate in the United States (although not all cultures and countries use the same gestures and, if so, they may not have the same meaning). A thumb pointed up often means "well done!" A thumb pointed down often means some kind of disappointment. An index finger (with palm up) pointing from another person to you often means "come here." An index finger (with palm down) and shaking from side to side often means "no" or "stop." A pinky in the air may be part of a discussion about keeping a promise ("pinky swear"). Of course, many children know that the middle finger has its own message, at times!

Style of Dress and Grooming

According to an old Russian proverb, "When a man enters a room, he is judged by how he dresses. When he leaves a room, he is judged by his wits." In other words, before someone gets to know your personality, they make a judgment about who you are on the basis of appearances. These initial, superficial conclusions are often wrong, but they can have a powerful impact on how others view a person. Using kid-friendly words, this is an important lesson to teach your children, even if they are teenagers.

Many parents of teenagers have felt frustrated when their requests for their adolescent to dress in certain ways in certain settings are ignored. The time to impress on children the following is when they are young:

- Clean clothes communicate a message. Dirty or smelly clothes also communicate a message.
- Wrinkled clothes versus wrinkle-free clothes affect how a person might be viewed.

- Mismatched versus coordinated clothing can create an impression on others (e.g., sometimes mismatched is in style, so it's important to check before assuming it's a lack of appreciation for color coordination).
- Many outfits are okay for particular settings and not a good fit for other settings (e.g., wearing a bathing suit to school, formal vs. informal wear).
- Certain styles communicate certain attitudes or messages (e.g., short skirts, pants below the underwear line).
- Slogans on clothing can allow others to know one's interests and can lead to conversations or to judgments.
- When a child dresses like a particular group (e.g., Goth, a particular group of athletes, a gang), it should be discussed because of the potential social reactions of adults and even peers.
- Of course, in the teen years, tattoos, body piercing, and coloring one's hair also communicate information about a person.

When you were young, did you ever have disagreements with your parents about how you looked when you walked out of your home? If so, you are not alone; it has been an age-old, exasperating discussion in many homes. Each generation seems to disapprove or be concerned about the appearance of the younger generation! Sometimes this concern is valid, and sometimes it is unimportant. However, figuring out whether you need to intervene is important.

When 11-year-old Kaitlyn insisted on wearing shorts to school when the outside temperature was just above freezing, her parents initially insisted that she change. However, when they saw other students at the bus stop, they were surprised to see that all but one child were wearing shorts. Kaitlyn later talked with her mother about why she made the decision to wear shorts that morning.

Kaitlyn: The bus is, like, 100 degrees. It drops us off at school, and the classroom is, like, 100 degrees too. Wearing shorts makes sense!

Mother: Okay. I guess it makes sense. But are you planning on wearing shorts when we go to the football game next week?

Kaitlyn: Get serious, Mom. That would just be weird! I'd freeze to death!

Kaitlyn's mother relaxed and realized she had been worried unnecessarily about the issue of Kaitlyn wearing shorts. The fact that both Kaitlyn and her mother took the time to talk to each other about Kaitlyn's decision helped them both avoid future disagreements on this same issue.

On a cold, snowy day, Andrew insisted on going to school without a jacket. After a futile discussion, his father said, "I give up. If that's what you want, go ahead." Five minutes later, when the bus had not yet arrived, Andrew loudly knocked at the door and shouted, "I'm freezing. Let me in. I need my jacket!" Andrew had a life lesson, and his father successfully withheld his temptation to say, "I told you so!"

What if you feel that your child is making a social faux pas that will likely lead to social rejection and negative judgments from others? With all the messages your children intentionally or accidentally share through their style of dress and grooming, it can often be difficult for parents to convince them about the messages they may be sending.

Children often become emotional when parents question their grooming or style of dressing. They have reported feeling rejected and judged by their parent, even when the parent is trying to be supportive and guide them. Despite how your child reacts, as the parent, you may need to try to protect her from some serious reactions from others (e.g., short shorts and a tight shirt worn with an exposed belly button by your developing tween daughter as she heads out the door for school). It's sometimes necessary to intervene.

Parents have found the following information beneficial when trying to guide their children:

- Screaming to be heard often leads children to tune parents out.
- An angry parent may be judged as overreacting by their children.
- You can often use logic rather than anger to have kids draw correct conclusions.
- Offer your child options (e.g., "If you want to go to this fancy restaurant with us and your grandparents, you'll have to wear nice pants and an appropriate shirt. If you don't want to, that's okay. You can stay home").
- If there are rules in the community that involve safety (e.g., wearing a helmet when riding a bicycle) you can still review options (e.g., "You can wear the helmet and ride or not wear the helmet and not ride. Which is more important to you?").

If you aren't sure whether you are overreacting, or even under-reacting, it's okay to ask the opinion of other parents or relatives whose judgment you trust. Raising kids is not always black and white, right or wrong. However, you may be relieved to know that the way children dress is most likely a temporary phase and unlikely to continue into adulthood; therefore, if your child starts to fight you, you may not want to pursue that battle. Of course, if the potential consequence is significant or even dangerous, you will have to take a stand and stick to it.

If you have open lines of communication with your child, discussing her style of dressing, words she uses for communicating, and even the texts she sends to friends may still create tension and disagreements. If, however, you do not feel you have open communication with your child, try some of the strategies listed earlier and start discussing how others (e.g., famous people) dress and what message that sends. This can be a nonthreatening way to begin the discussion about how physical appearance communicates certain messages.

TRYING TOO HARD CAN BACKFIRE

You may have known a child like Warren. He desperately wanted to be accepted by the fifth-grade kids who were popular and on the soccer team. Warren tried to get on the travel soccer team with these boys, but the coach didn't think he was good enough. Warren tried to sit with these boys at lunch, even though they gave him no indication they wanted him there. He brought in a soccer ball and offered to play with them at recess. When none of them accepted his offer, he just stood near them and played with his ball as they played with another one.

After a few weeks of this behavior, Warren was no closer to gaining acceptance. The boys started referring to him as a "wannabe" behind his back. They also laughed at how "desperate" he was to join them. Soon the team members started pretending to like him to get him to do things for them (e.g., homework, getting their lunch for them from the lunch line), while behind his back they continued to make fun of him.

There are many boys and girls who are determined to gain inclusion into a particular group of children. These children may have been taught the value of hard work. However, when a child appears to be trying too hard or is overeager or overanxious to join a group, other children can find it annoying and want nothing to do with this child. At other times, the overeager child also tries to gain acceptance by trying to sound extremely knowledgeable or even superior. These children are at risk of being labeled "know-it-alls." Trying to fit in with a group by using humor can sometimes backfire as well. Humor that works with one group of children or adults may not work with another group. It can also be problematic to be viewed as the "class clown." Ah, it is not easy to be a child!

If you notice your child is working hard to be accepted by a group that is not the right match for him, it's important to let him know that

- just because this particular group isn't welcoming him, it does not mean that there is something wrong with him;
- working hard is great when the goal is realistic;
- if he has to try constantly to impress others, there is a problem because the other kids probably aren't impressed; and
- if he has to pretend he is someone different than who he is, it's the wrong group for him.

Some well-intentioned parents have seen the pain their children encounter when working hard to fit in with a group only to be rejected. The parents may think they are helping their children by intervening with the parents of children who are in the desired group or by forbidding their children from hanging out with the group. However, children (and certainly teenagers) may see these parental responses as meaning that the parent doesn't understand, and the children may think they can't share their feelings and intense "need" with them any longer. It's important to make sure communication is open so children can share their struggles with trusted adults. Furthermore, if you did call the parents of a child in the desired group, and ask them to speak to their son or daughter about letting your child be included, this can backfire by upsetting the parent and irritating both your child and the other child. Another unfortunate potential consequence is that your child may be more vulnerable to being teased because of your phone call.

YOUR CHILD'S RESPONSE TO SOCIAL REJECTION

When children believe they are outcasts or rejected by peers, it can be a huge blow to their self-confidence. Your child may be verbal and confide in you about this situation. However, other children sometimes react to this experience with behavioral and emotional changes. A child may not talk at all about it but become more emotional or temperamental. Another child may act out in defiant or other angry ways. Of course, each child is different, but if you see changes in how your child is acting or reacting, it's worth trying to figure out whether he has been experiencing social rejection.

There are some key ways to help children become resilient by dealing with and moving past the rejection. Lessons are best learned when the rejection is minor, and children are not overwhelmed with their emotions. For instance, Keya is 8 years old. She came home from a play date and heard through the closed bedroom door of her older sister's room that her sister was talking and laughing with friends. Keya wanted to join them and politely knocked on the door. When her sister opened it, Keya asked, "What's up?" as she walked in and sat down on her sister's bed. Keya's sister, age 12, immediately told Keya, "Get out of here. We don't want little kids hanging around us right now." Keya looked at her sister's friends, hoping they would say she could stay. The friends just stared at her. Keya left after this rejection and felt dejected as well as angry. She ran to her mother, crying and complaining about her treatment.

Keya's mother tried to soothe her daughter and used this opportunity to discuss ways to deal with feelings of rejection. Her mother used the following steps to help Keya to gain coping strategies:

- She made sure Keya was calm and emotionally able to have a discussion about what occurred.
- She asked Keya to describe what happened, from her perspective.

169

- She asked Keya to describe what happened, from her sister's perspective.
- She asked Keya to think about whether her sister rejected her request or rejected her.
- She asked Keya to think about what she would have done if her 4-year-old brother wanted to join her when she had friends over.
- She asked Keya whether she would have changed her actions if she could do the situation over again.

When Keya's mother pointed out that Keya had responded similarly when her younger brother intruded on her play dates, Keya recognized that sometimes siblings want to just be with friends of their own age. Because Keya and her mother had a close, loving, and supportive connection, it was easier for Keya to be open to having this discussion, and she was comforted by it.

If children have self-confidence, they are more likely to bounce back from rejection and look for others who accept them. When a child says, "What's wrong with me? Why don't those kids like me?" it's a time for a serious parent–child discussion. This comment implies that this child doesn't feel valuable if he is not accepted by the peer group. During the parent–child discussion, it is important to spend time having your child reflect on his areas of strength and what he takes pride in about himself. Emphasizing the talents, abilities, skills, and special qualities of your child may help raise his confidence level and self-esteem and allow him to bounce back from the rejection and refocus his energy on looking for friends who appreciate him for being him.

The following ideas can help children remember their value, even in the face of rejection, and get through stressful times.

- From the start of life, giving the consistent and repeated message to your child that she is valued, valuable, and enjoyable can create a foundation for resiliency.

- Being accepted by both parents is extremely important in fostering a sense of security and self-worth in children.
- Use some of the strategies you read about earlier in this book for fostering frustration tolerance, problem-solving skills, and confidence.
- Point out that others appreciate your child, even though one group may not (e.g., "Many kids like you, but it's okay if not all kids do").
- Discuss, when your child is calm, his or her personality and interests and how this information can point the way to a particular group of friends.
- Ask your child what she would say to herself right now if she were a supportive best friend to herself.
- Ask your child why this group seems so important.
- After all this discussion, it's time for a hug, then a break and distraction (e.g., a fun activity, a chance for your child to laugh again and realize that it's possible!).

There are times when adults can help children resolve disagreements. For instance, if you and your best friend realize that your children are rejecting one another, you could plan a structured play date when both children focus on an activity (e.g., doing an art project) and happen to learn to appreciate each other. However, calling up a parent and complaining that their child is rejecting or bullying your child (see the next section) can often backfire.

COPING WITH BULLYING BEHAVIORS AND UNINTENTIONAL BULLYING

The topic of bullying receives a great deal of coverage in the media. Parents are often anxious about the possibility of their child being bullied. Some parents are also nervous that they might be called into school to see the principal because their child is bullying others.

Bullying occurs when there is an imbalance of power, and the more powerful child purposely picks on a more vulnerable child. This can occur face-to-face, by telephone messages, or even by using social media (cyberbullying). Unfortunately, there are some children who are mislabeled as bullies when they are inappropriately trying to lead or engage in some age-typical teasing.

If you hear that your child is being bullied, the following are some questions to think about and responses that might help:

- Is the issue actually about bullying or is it about assertiveness (e.g., "Harry always tells me what to do"). If you determine that it's about assertiveness, role-play respectful but clear responses that your child can use for this situation and can be generalized to future situations. Sometimes an assertive friend makes decisions for a more passive friend to help that child out rather than to bully him.
- If someone is teasing your child, ask whether your child believes the other person knows that it is upsetting her. Sometimes just telling another child your feelings are hurt can end the teasing when it was never intended to make anyone uncomfortable.
- Get the specific details about how long it has been going on, what the bullying involves, and who witnesses it. This information will help you come up with a way to help your child.
- Find out what your child has already done to try to deal with the situation.
- Without blaming the target (your child), ask how your child and the other person relate to each other and what your child has done recently before or while this difficulty has been occur-

ring. Please know that it's never advisable to blame the target. This questioning is more for the purpose of clarification than assigning blame.

The person who is on the receiving end of bullying is generally referred to as a *target*, not as a *victim*, because he generally has some choices in what to do. If your child is a target, he or she has options. This is important for your child to learn. The following are some key points to share with your child:

- It's more difficult for another child to bully someone who is in a group of supportive others. Therefore, encourage your child to stay with an accepting group who will stand by your child if a bully starts to try to make her or him feel uncomfortable.
- Sometimes bullying continues because it's "entertaining." This means that the target reacts strongly. Depending on the situation, sometimes ignoring or shrugging one's shoulders and walking away is the best approach.
- If it's safe, there are ways to strike back verbally (see the upcoming example).
- If children feel victimized, it's important for them to know they can talk with and get support, guidance, and help from trusted adults or older sensible siblings.
- If the bullying is potentially dangerous (e.g., your child is at risk of being physically assaulted; your child becomes clinically depressed, anxious, or school phobic), it's important for children to immediately seek safety and speak with an adult.

Children often report that they feel they should always deal with tough situations on their own. Therefore, parents should discuss the fact that children, and even adults, sometimes need help in dealing with situations that create feelings of fear or cause them to experience emotional and/or physical pain. The life lesson here is that we all need help sometimes, and it's a sign of strength, not weakness, to ask for it when it is truly needed. Once you hear the concerns, you can decide whether it's time to speak with the school administrators, staff, or on rare occasions, the police.

Samuel, at the age of 10, was verbally bullied and felt intimidated by Matt, who was taller, larger, and more popular. Samuel never felt physically threatened but felt angry, embarrassed, and humiliated. At first, he didn't know what to do and often tried to stay home, feigning illness. After he had confided his troubles to his 15-year-old brother, Samuel felt he had some verbal tools to deal with the situation. The next time Matt picked on him, Samuel looked him directly in the eye and said, "Matt, does it make you feel good to pick on someone smaller than you?" When Matt smiled, looked at his friends, and said, "Yeah!" Samuel was ready. He looked at Matt's friends and said, "Do all of you enjoy this? Get a life and leave me alone!" Samuel held his breath and waited. If that line didn't work, he had other strategies. However, Samuel was rewarded when one of Matt's friends spoke to Matt and said, "He's not worth your energy. Let's go." Throughout school, Samuel never forgot the strategies he learned and the feeling of success he gained from his encounter with Matt. He gained confidence to speak up and not be intimidated, and he more deeply appreciated the power of speech and the value of being accepted by peers. Samuel ended up becoming an upstander for others.

If your child is bullied, you can use the situation as an opportunity to brainstorm ways to handle it. Frequently, older siblings can also add advice in these times. However, even if your child disagrees, mes also need advice on how to support your child and r her safety.

Raising an Upstander

An *upstander* is someone who stands up for what is right when witnessing injustices. It is not always easy to be an upstander. These individuals are sometimes also referred to as *positive bystanders*. Upstanders do not necessarily have to put themselves in harm's way, but make decisions to intervene or actively seek others who can help when needed.

There are numerous prerequisites to becoming an upstander. The person has to recognize a problem is occurring, has to have the commitment to right injustices and the courage to do so, has to have the knowledge of how to handle the situation, and has to have the common sense to know whether it is a wise plan. It may be easier for an outgoing, confident person to become an upstander, but that is not necessary in all cases. There are times when an upstander is not particularly confident, and is even scared about stepping in, but his sense of right and wrong allows him to overcome fears.

The following are some ways parents have encouraged their children to grow into becoming upstanders:

- Read stories with your child that encourage prosocial and even courageous actions.
- Model standing up for what is right and knowing when to "stand down" or not intervene.
- Offer praise when your child does stand up for what is right.
- Encourage your child to talk with you about situations he witnesses and to which he isn't sure how to respond.
- It can be helpful to role-play how some situations can be handled. This allows your child to learn the possible verbal responses to diffuse a conflict.
- Discuss how simply saying to the target, "Hey, we're late for our meeting with the teacher to work on the project" can get the target out of the bullying situation.

- Discuss when it's important not to intervene directly but to get help from an adult (e.g., what they can say to that adult).
- When your child becomes a preteen, it can be helpful to discuss the reports of ways bystanders chose to respond (by not responding) while the Kitty Genovese murder occurred in 1964 and how we have learned valuable lessons from this.

Other children are *neutral bystanders*, which means they may watch but do nothing. There are also *negative bystanders*, who may laugh or in other purposeful or accidental ways encourage the bullying. It is important to know that some children who laugh or act like negative bystanders may be as upset with the situation as the upstander is but are afraid to intervene and simultaneously display nervous laughter as opposed to supportive laughter. Helping these children discuss their reaction and learn ways to become upstanders can increase their self-confidence and self-worth. The upstander usually feels a sense of pride after trying to do what he deems is important, even if the outcome isn't immediately successful.

Hearing That Your Child is Bullying

Imagine getting a phone call from your child's school to tell you that your child has been bullying another student. Parents can experience a multitude of reactions from embarrassment to astonishment to disbelief to anger at the caller, to anger and disappointment with their child. Before drawing any conclusions, it can be helpful to set up a meeting with the school staff to get more information so you can have a clearer understanding of the situation and find out whether your child is truly bullying or being misperceived as engaging in this behavior. Before your meeting, however, it's important to sit down with your child and listen to his side of the story without judging. Of course, many children work hard to avoid disappointing parents, so you may get the story they prefer you to hear rather than the factual details.

It is not uncommon for a child to be misperceived as bullying. If this describes your child, it's important to work with your child and the school staff to correct this. Some children engage in behaviors that are more assertive, but because they are popular with many friends who encourage the actions, more vulnerable students feel powerless in their presence. This isn't only about helping the powerless children but also the assertive ones to consider the feelings of others.

However, if you find that your child is bullying, it's time to quickly intervene so that others are no longer hurt and your child's reputation improves. Donna, age 10, was an outgoing, confident, and popular leader of a small group of girls. She often joked with her friends and with close acquaintances. One fellow student, Madelaine, often smiled when Donna teased her. Donna thought Madelaine enjoyed the jokes. Madelaine, however, went home crying daily, stating that Donna is "so mean. She makes fun of me all the time."

When the teacher and the parents of both girls investigated, it turned out that Donna's behaviors were truly having a negative impact on Madelaine. However, all agreed that Madelaine's reactions led Donna to believe her words were harmless. This is not to blame Madelaine but to understand the situation better.

Once Donna learned the true impact her words had on Madelaine, she willingly apologized and stopped teasing her. Donna learned that not everybody has the same sense of humor. She was more cautious about teasing peers after this incident, having learned that not all students will share their true reaction to teasing. Madelaine entered into short-term counseling and worked on developing more resiliency skills, such as ways to respond to unwelcome comments or teasing from others.

Unfortunately, there are some children who purposely bully others. There are many reasons (e.g., emotional, environmental, life experiences) why a child chooses to pick on other children. It is serious, though, if your child bullies and does not respond to intervention. Deeper reasons behind his or her actions should be explored along with the consequences that have been effective for other children who display this behavior.

Whether your child is a target, an unintentional bully, or acting like a bully, the situation must be addressed. If a simple and direct approach to rectifying the situation does not work, it is important to include other adults in seeking solutions. At times, a child benefits from self-reflection and skill building under the guidance of a mental health professional who has experience in this area.

SUMMARY

In this chapter, you read about various topics related to social interactions, including knowing how voice tone, body language, and choice of words can affect others. In addition, ways to help children to become upstanders and the topic of bullying were addressed. In the next chapter, various challenges of raising a child in the computer generation, including the problem of cyberbullying, are explored.

CHAPTER 8

INDEPENDENT TECHNOLOGY USE: TEACHING CHILDREN ABOUT THE RISKS AND BENEFITS

For good or bad, beneficial or harmful, technology is here to stay. As with many other advances, how it is used determines how useful and helpful it can be. Technology includes many functions that are used daily, such as texting, surfing the web, engaging in online education, having a conference with colleagues from a variety of locations, doing surgery using robotics, or driving one's car (or even riding in a driverless car!). It can sometimes be tricky to not only monitor your child's activities on electronics but also to convince him that you may know best even though he may be more technologically sophisticated.

In this chapter, we discuss the risks of children using excessive and/or uncensored technology and interacting on social media. In addition, we address some social and legal ramifications of particular behaviors online. Of course, there are many ways children can benefit from technology, and we explore some of these as well.

Before reading further, take a minute to reflect on how you foster your child's appropriate use of the computer in and outside your home.

For each item listed below, fill in the number that corresponds best to your response:

(continues)

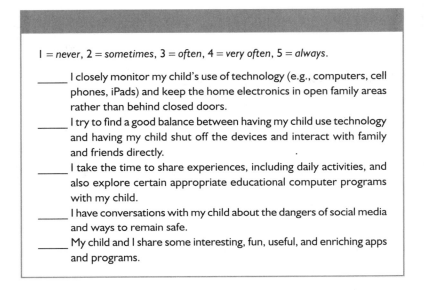

1 = *never*, 2 = *sometimes*, 3 = *often*, 4 = *very often*, 5 = *always*.

_____ I closely monitor my child's use of technology (e.g., computers, cell phones, iPads) and keep the home electronics in open family areas rather than behind closed doors.

_____ I try to find a good balance between having my child use technology and having my child shut off the devices and interact with family and friends directly.

_____ I take the time to share experiences, including daily activities, and also explore certain appropriate educational computer programs with my child.

_____ I have conversations with my child about the dangers of social media and ways to remain safe.

_____ My child and I share some interesting, fun, useful, and enriching apps and programs.

Children who are growing up in today's world have an advantage if they are comfortable using technology. However, parents of children growing up in today's world face many challenges and can feel uncomfortable when they are not able to entirely monitor their child's Internet and social media site activities. Of course, most parents appreciate the fact that there are some significant technological advances, such as in the medical field. Technology has helped the disabled become more able, such as hearing aids, cochlear implants, computer guided radiation therapy, and so forth. In this chapter, you will read about the benefits of technology for children and ways you can ponder and react to the risks.

ADVANTAGES TECHNOLOGY OFFERS STUDENTS FOR SCHOOL

Most children can come up with many reasons they need their computer, iPad, or phone. Their reasons are often accurate, although they are only part of the story of how technology affects them. Let's explore the advantages.

In school, your child may have one or more computer terminals or iPads in the classroom. Computers are frequently used during class time when students are researching topics, creating presentations (e.g., PowerPoint, Prezi), and typing essays. There are even kid-friendly educational games on the computer (e.g., math activities) that students can play to reinforce their knowledge of subject areas. It can be helpful if you know how to use these programs as well. Ask your child to share her knowledge and the way technology supports her learning in school.

At home, technology is often important when students are working in a group to complete homework. There are numerous programs, such as Google Docs, that help children work together on group projects over the Internet. Students may use FaceTime, Skype, or other programs to work together in a—hopefully—productive way. Group chats are a great way for students to be part of a study group even when they are in their own homes.

Mary, age 11, has grown up with computers and iPads and knows how to navigate around the web. In school, she has learned and knows how to use a variety of techniques to show her knowledge when she is asked to do a presentation or group project. When she recently had to do a class presentation about Abraham Lincoln, she used the computer to

- research his early years;
- research his character throughout the years;
- research the time he lived in history (during the Civil War) and how his actions affected the course of the war and the abolition of slavery;
- research his presidency and assassination;
- create a PowerPoint presentation that emphasized the points she researched and was going to talk about in class;

- download pictures relevant to each point and put them into the slides to add interest;
- upload a voice-over for a few slides in which she recorded her older brother as Lincoln sharing perceptions of events he lived through; and
- Skype her uncle, who loves history, to run through her speech with him the week before her presentation. He had many positive comments and a few suggestions.

When Mary was working on her school assignment, she displayed many of the important skills you read about in Chapter 3. There are some children who seem to develop these independent skills naturally and are motivated to complete their responsibilities. They know how to blend research, use technology with executive functioning skills, and add artistic (e.g., graphs, pictures) displays to highlight points.

Mary, however, was not initially one of these organized students who combined the variety of skills needed to create a cohesive, comprehensive, and clear presentation. Even with the use of the computer, a child does not magically become organized, know how to persevere at a task, and figure out how to prioritize what material to include or exclude. Children also don't magically know about copyrights, intellectual property, and the risk of accidental plagiarism and when it's necessary to seek permission to use certain materials. Take time to consider whether your child needs support in developing these abilities, both when using a computer to complete tasks and when doing other kinds of work.

The earlier you and the classroom teachers can start helping your child become self-sufficient in using the positive functions technology offers (e.g., editing and organizing work; combining words, images, or even music) and combining these with the executive functioning skills she can apply to many other aspects of her life, the easier it will be for your child to feel confident as she presents well-developed projects. Of course, parental monitoring of what children do on the Internet is important and is explored later in this chapter.

Mary, with encouragement from her parents, persevered, was organized, set aside some time each evening to work on the project, broke down the assignment into smaller segments to work on so she avoided being overwhelmed, and maintained her motivation to do a thorough project. Mary told her mother that without computer access, "This would have taken me forever. I learned so much and so quickly by checking out websites instead of having to read through a million books!" Mary's ability to take advantage of many informative and relevant websites, easily integrate the facts she learned, and edit her presentation using the computer reflects how useful technology can be in education.

Computers can also be helpful when a child has special learning needs or prefers a certain learning style. For example, a visual learner can watch educational videos online to summarize points made by the teacher in the classroom. A child who has fine-motor issues (e.g., effectively using a pen or pencil) can sometimes use a keyboard more easily. There are even programs that allow students to dictate information or essays into a word processing program. Many of these accommodations would need the approval of your child's teacher and should not be used as a crutch but rather as a support when necessary.

Other advantages of technology include your children's ability to contact you via cell phone while they are at school and cannot locate a landline. A quick text can let you know when your child has to be picked up. Children can even type short notes into their phone to remind themselves of assignments or to do certain tasks.

The information now at children's fingertips is truly amazing. Within a few seconds, many children can find out information on topics of interest, can text without focusing on conventional spelling, and can have access to a wide variety of apps and games. However, the downside of technology becomes apparent if children never learn to research topics when a computer is not available, never focus on conventional spelling because it's not needed while texting, or become enthralled with age-inappropriate games.

ADVANTAGES TECHNOLOGY OFFERS CHILDREN IN THEIR SOCIAL LIVES

There has been a lot of media coverage of the risks arising from children's interactions with others while using their electronic devices. These concerns are highlighted later in this chapter. However, connecting with others on one's electronic devices can have positive outcomes as well.

Sending Quick Texts

Think back to the "old days" when a person had to find a phone, often connected to the wall by a wire, to make contact with others who were not right there. You may have encountered a busy signal, endless ringing without an answering machine available, and much frustration. In today's world, children can often send and receive texts anytime and anywhere they have cell service. That means your child can send you a quick text to ask you whether a friend can come over or text one or more friends and schedule a get-together. The receivers of your text may not be able to chat at that moment and sometimes may not be able to read your text immediately, but the text remains there waiting to be read.

In some neighborhoods, much of the social planning may be done by texting. In this situation, children who lack the ability to receive texts have to find ways to learn about the social activities friends are planning (e.g., by asking a friend to let them know the plans). If you do not feel your child is old enough to need a phone or you cannot afford to get him one, it's important to guide him on how to stay connected to other kids in the many available ways, such as calling on the home phone, speaking at school, and so forth.

Socializing When Get-Togethers Aren't Possible

As you probably know, as your children get older and eventually become teenagers, their friends become an increasingly important part of their daily lives. This focus on peers is natural and often a step forward as children move toward independence. However, parents may experience anxiety when this occurs, hoping that the peer group will be a positive influence but fearing that it may not.

When friends can't get together, they often have the capability to socialize via the Internet. It can frustrate parents when their children are at home but are not focused on or participating in family activities. When children focus too much on social media, it can have drawbacks, but in moderation, it can have numerous advantages.

You can decide where your children use their technology, and this can then give you the opportunity to monitor it more easily. For example, Dennis, age 10, loved group chats with his friends. His parents allowed this but set house rules, which included the hours he could do this, the behaviors and words they expected him to use, and that he had to be in the family room whenever this occurred. One of his parents would plan to walk into the room at random times to make sure the chats were appropriate and positive. During the rare moments they were uncomfortable with part of the conversation, they did not interject their disapproval or concern at that time so as not to embarrass Dennis. Rather, they made sure to use this as a "teachable moment" later that evening.

Socializing over the Internet by Skyping or FaceTime, for example, can help children

- figure out when to speak and when to listen in a group,
- listen for voice intonations to hear the intent behind messages,
- pick up on the local slang for that age group, and
- keep updated on the latest news others are sharing.

If your child or tween wants to socialize via the Internet, there are risks, which we discuss shortly. However, the following are some ideas to consider if you allow this access:

- Not all video games are appropriate for all ages. Because playing video games with others is a popular activity, spend some time reviewing the game and discussing the theme and whether you will allow it to be played before your child is already interacting with peers.
- If you decide a video game is inappropriate and should not be played, explain your rationale to your child so it's not viewed as a random decision or attempt to control his every action.
- Some parents find it helpful to place cell phones in a basket in the kitchen so that all socializing with others is done via computer or iPad in a set location that parents can monitor.
- Consider setting times when your child can have access to her electronics or technology so she also has time to focus on being with family, socializing with peers in person, and completing other responsibilities (e.g., chores, homework).
- Review your expectations regarding your child's behaviors when on the computer (of course, this is important when they are in any situation). For some children, having them sign a contract in which the rules are stated clearly can be useful.

- If your child disagrees with your rules, listen, decide whether you should compromise, and then let your child know your final decision. If she disobeys, let her know the consequence and ask her to rethink her stance. The consequence may be to use the computer only for school and when you are present. You may feel that additional consequences may be needed, but make sure your child knows how to regain her technology privileges.
- Review with your child the permanence of texts, cyberbullying, and legal consequences of the misuse of technology so she doesn't make an accidental but serious mistake (you could also check with your child's school to see how students have been educated already on this topic).
- Depending on your child, consider the appropriate balance between monitoring and giving your child privacy.

Socializing over the Internet, when it's done responsibly, can be an advantage, especially when a child is home sick or can't get together with others because of inclement weather. Many adults have also discovered the benefits of technology at these times. Having access to friends can help minimize cabin fever, whether you're a child or a parent!

For many decades, long-term connections with distant friends and family were maintained through letter writing, phone calls, and periodic visits. Nowadays, face-to-face contact over the Internet allows people to see facial expressions and body language. In addition, this technology makes it possible for a person to show his friend or relative something specific or introduce someone to them (e.g., Brett showed his friend how he decorated his new room and introduced him to his new dog). At times, students have even connected with fellow students who live far away.

Sharing Common Experiences

As your child grows, having friends and common experiences with same-age peers can foster a sense of security and belonging and provide knowledge about how others are going through the particular developmental stages, even if it's not ever talked about. Jokes, interests, and activities shared among friends can not only be enjoyable but can also lead your child to realize she can sometimes be safe and have fun without your supervision. If there is a group chat that resembles kids just "hanging out," it may be a way for kids to feel included in their social circle. Although getting together is an important part of socializing, being connected with friends via social media can also lead to social interactions and keeping up with current trends, and it can simply be fun.

Although you may approve of your child's talking with friends over social media, you may have more concerns about your child's playing video games. Some parents have banned such games entirely. However, if your child is not familiar with video games or websites that are parent approved and frequented by peers, he may feel left out. Therefore, when trying to figure out what to allow your child to view or do on the Internet, these are important points to consider and talk about with him.

There are other ways that using technology can foster common experiences or increase the ease of communication. Imagine if your family had just moved to America and your child was unfamiliar with the English language. She or he may still be able to connect with peers by nonverbal communication, but there are limitations. By using an app, a child may be able to have her words translated so other children can understand what is being said. In addition, children who relocate can still maintain face-to-face contact, over the Internet, with old friends and family so they don't feel entirely disconnected.

Despite all the advantages of living in a technologically sophisticated world, there are clearly some cautions and disadvantages. In the upcoming section, you have the opportunity to read about them.

DRAWBACKS OF INTERNET AND SOCIAL MEDIA USE FOR KIDS

You may have grown up in the world of technology and know how helpful it can be and also be aware of its drawbacks. In this section, you have the opportunity to think about ways to prevent, minimize, or simply monitor some of these risks and how they might affect your child.

As you set guidelines for how your child can use technology, remember to have discussions with your child about how and why you set these rules. By doing this, your child can become more aware of the issues and the risks, as well as benefits, of using computers wisely. At appropriate times, to build self-reflection and develop the ability to make sound choices when you are not present, you may want to guide your child but allow him to lead in decision making about his use of technology.

At School and With Schoolwork

In school and at home, adults generally set limits about when it's okay to use technology. Despite knowing these rules, children may be tempted to be on their phone, text, or play games at school. The immediate gratification of engaging in one of these activities at the wrong time or wrong place may supersede the focus on following the rules set by adults.

Christina, for example, at the age of 10 received a cell phone for her birthday. Within a few days she had downloaded several fun apps and was proficient at using the various functions of the phone. In school, Christina was a strong student and quickly grasped concepts

189

during lessons. She became bored once she understood the lesson and then turned to her cell phone to play games or text friends. She was not overtly disruptive but was distracted. One day, she lifted her head from her phone and realized her teacher had moved on to a new lesson, and she had missed the information entirely. Christina felt anxious about missing the material and worried about the next quiz.

Even adults, at business meetings, fall into the same trap as Christina. Boredom is sometimes hard to tolerate, especially when the alternative of using technology is available. For children, being able to tolerate some boredom, think about productive ways to decrease this boredom, and respectfully communicate their feelings to teachers are important skills for developing self-advocacy rather than choosing to withdraw into the world of the smartphone.

Teachers may take technology devices away from children if they are used during the school day. Check with your child's teachers or school administrators about school policies. There are numerous actions children might engage in with their phones at school that can lead to reprimands, consequences, and having their phones temporarily confiscated. Certainly, a child who takes a snapshot of the math test to share with friends who have the test later that day would not be considered to have engaged in an appropriate action. Texting during class can lead to children missing lessons, so it is also not viewed as appropriate. In addition, children have a right to be in school without having their picture taken (without giving permission). Yet, children with cameras on their phone may be tempted to do just that.

The following are some points to start discussions with your child about technology in school:

- Get a copy of the school's rules regarding technology, and discuss these rules with your child so he doesn't innocently (or intentionally) break a rule.

- Discuss the rationale behind some of the rules, such as focusing on the lesson, respecting those around you, or considering the appropriate etiquette of a particular situation.
- Discuss the personal consequences of missing out on a lesson (e.g., anxiety, lack of information).
- Discuss the additional consequences of losing the phone or iPad if it is used at the wrong time, in the wrong way, or in the wrong place.
- Model how you avoid taking out your phone, even when bored, if the time and place are not appropriate.

In addition to the social and behavioral issues related to using technology at school, there are also some academic disadvantages that emerge from overreliance on texting, for instance. There are many words used in texting that are not spelled in the traditional way. For instance, when Zev sent a text to his friend to ask a question, he wrote, "R u going 2 the party 2nite?" Now, imagine if he spelled those words in this fashion when writing an essay for class. Students usually know that spelling *are* as *R* is not conventional. However, they may not automatically remember that some text spelling is not traditional or accurate spelling for class assignments.

Using word processors can add another impediment to learning spelling and grammar skills. We often use spell-check and grammar check as backups to correct oversights when typing. However, some students depend so much on these that they don't develop the automaticity of spelling many words accurately on their own. Because your child will eventually be asked to write notes or comments at college or on the job without the benefit of spell-check, it's important for her to learn writing skills without constant reliance on the computer.

To build these abilities, you can do the following:

- Have conversations with your child about the benefits of the computer but also the necessity of knowing proper spelling and grammar rules (e.g., job interviews sometimes involve writing an answer to a presented question or dilemma right before one enters the interview room).
- Contact your child's teacher to see how you can support your child's development of these skills, independent of the computer.
- It may even help if your child sends "snail mail" to relatives, so he remains familiar with this means of communication and the skills needed for it.

There are several other costs to a child's overreliance on technology. Intellectually, if a child is a curious learner and searches out new information on the computer, it is a wonderful advantage of technology. However, if the same child does not know how to independently research information without the use of a computer, he may be disadvantaged when only books are available.

Stephen, age 11, for example, planned to complete a research project on Martin Luther King Jr. the weekend before it was due. He felt confident he could finish the project within this time frame. Unfortunately for Stephen, there was a major storm that Friday evening that caused a power outage all through Saturday and early Sunday morning. Stephen began to panic and told his father, "I'll never get the project done. I need the computer. Can you write a note to my teacher so I can get more time to do it?"

If you were Stephen's father, how would you have responded? Stephen was a victim of circumstances outside of his control (e.g., the storm, no power), but he was also a victim of his decision to wait until the last minute to do the assignment. In addition, he was at a disadvantage because he did not think about using encyclopedias or checking whether there was a book on Martin Luther King Jr. in the family's extensive book collection.

Stephen's father thought he had several options to help his son, including (a) writing a note to the teacher asking for an extension of the due date for Stephen; (b) telling Stephen to use the books in the home; (c) telling Stephen that because he waited too long, he now had to face the consequences at school; and (d) using this opportunity to help Stephen improve his time-management skills and learn how to do research and write papers without the use of his computer.

Stephen's father chose options b and d. Because Stephen was nervous about not having a completed assignment by the due date, he was receptive, at that moment, to his father's guidance. Stephen's father felt a great deal of pleasure about sharing his knowledge with his receptive son. Stephen did not ever want to feel this uncomfortable again, waiting until the last minute or relying so much on technology. Therefore, despite his preference to have his father fix the situation rather than use it as a teaching tool, Stephen reluctantly listened to his father and began to view books as a suitable backup if the computer was not available when he wanted to research a topic. Years later, Stephen still remembers his father's lessons and now uses the knowledge independently.

At Home

There are many 2-year-olds who understand the basics of how to use their parents' phone or computer to play games. This is a remarkable sign of the capacity of young children to learn and use this information. As children get a little older, computer games are sometimes used as "babysitters" while the parent is busy with anoth activity. However, there comes a time when using this techn' can have minor or even major drawbacks.

For instance, when a child is on her iPad or computer for long periods playing games that involve sitting and staring at a screen, rather than running around outside, it can lead to weight gain, social isolation, eye strain, or lack of development of other skills. There are also some significant concerns for children when they use a device for listening to music with earbuds. When the volume is high and the music is delivered directly to the ears by earbuds, some of these young users experience hearing difficulties.

Another drawback of growing up in the world of technology is that some children rarely see coins or bills. For instance, Jacqueline always knew that you pay for items by swiping a card through a machine or handing the card to a salesperson. Her parents prided themselves in never carrying around cash. Even when Jacqueline was old enough to go shopping with friends, her mother gave her a credit card (and letter of permission to use it). Unfortunately, this consistent use of "plastic" deprived Jacqueline of the opportunity to learn about coins and bills. In fact, she never learned to budget, thinking the card was an endless invitation to spend. Discussions about credit cards, debit cards, and cash are important for children to have with parents so they are prepared to use all these options, and sensibly, when they are older.

MONITORING YOUR CHILD'S COMPUTER AND INTERNET USE

Throughout this chapter, you have read about the benefits of monitoring your child's computer use. Children sometimes generalize face-to-face communication skills into the world of online communication, such as texting or sending e-mails. It is helpful if you take time to discuss the fact that in e-mails or texting, the receiver of the message can misperceive the sender's intent because of the lack of voice intonation or body language. Another person may think your child is serious when your child is making a joke. Imagine the communication issues that can arise from that! Friendships can be lost because of these misunderstandings.

In addition, communication over the Internet can lead to difficulties because it is generally part of a permanent record and can be shared with others whom your child may never have intended to be included in the conversation. The serious topics of stranger danger (addressed later in this chapter) and cyberbullying require special attention so your child does not innocently face either issue. When it comes to both of these situations, open communication with parents has helped many children avoid victimization or enabled them to correct a situation in which they were perceived as cyberbullying another person.

Cyberbullying

In the last chapter, we discussed the topic of bullying. When bullying occurs via the Internet, it's labeled *cyberbullying*. Although the information shared in Chapter 7 offered guidance for dealing with bullying, unique issues arise in cyberbullying. For example, the "bully" never comes face-to-face with the target (sometimes referred to as the *victim*). In addition, harsh words or even demeaning pictures can be quickly and easily forwarded to many people, both those with whom the aggressor wanted to share and those who were not intended to receive the message, because others can forward the item to more people.

If you learn that your child is using technology to hurt another child, the same discussions from the last chapter apply here. However, for cyberbullying, the following are a few important additional pointers:

- Education is key (e.g., it's recorded permanently; others can be seriously hurt, and you may not even know it; it can be detrimental to you in the future; there are some legal ramifications to cyberbullying).

- Discuss ways to rectify the situation, if possible.
- In life there are consequences, so if your child has misused technology, consider revoking the privilege of Internet access for a prescribed period.

There are times when a child sends a hurtful message to another child with the intent of being sarcastic. However, without the voice intonation (as previously discussed), the sarcastic meaning is lost, and the words may be taken literally. In addition, if the sender of the aggressive message means to make someone feel only a little uncomfortable, there is no immediate way to know whether the receiver of the message is devastated, annoyed, or anxious or whether he thought the message was simply meant to be funny.

If your child is accused of cyberbullying, this information may be shared with the school, and the school may investigate. These days, when some children have killed themselves because of feeling victimized, many adults try to deal quickly with true bullying, whether it is face-to-face or via the Internet. It can be emotionally disturbing to get a phone call from your child's school because your child has engaged in cyberbullying. If this should happen to you, first take a second to breathe! Next, try to learn as many facts as you can so you can have a discussion about it with your child. Then, you can follow up with the school staff or others who are experienced with how to deal with these conflictual situations and are, most often, there to support children and resolve the issue.

An individual involved in cyberbullying is called the *bully*, *aggressor*, or *perpetrator*. Sometimes these children just need edu-
⸱ ⸱ ʾels because they never meant to hurt another per-
l have to learn from the unintentional results of

The receiver of cyberbullying is often labeled as the *victim* or *target*. Victims are usually now referred to as *targets* because these individuals often have some options for handling the situation rather than simply being passive recipients.

If you learn that your child is a target of cyberbullying, the following are a few important suggestions:

- Ask your child to save the message to show you, even though she may be embarrassed by it and want to make it disappear by deleting it.
- Ask your child how the message made her feel, then listen without judging and explore why the message led to those particular feelings.
- If you feel that the message is meant to be hurtful, talk with your child about the relationship with the sender and ask whether this is the first such message of this kind.
- If the message does not upset your child that much, does not directly threaten your child or others, the sender has not engaged in such behavior in the past, and your child wants to respond, you can act as a coach rather than immediately and directly intervening. However, it's important for you to continue to monitor any future messages to see whether the negative messages continue.
- If you act as a coach, encourage your child to avoid getting into lengthy discussions with the sender. Discuss the benefits of a quick response versus ignoring the message. The importance of your child choosing friends who share common values and interests and who also have respect for each other is especially important to reinforce at this time.
- Last, talk with your child about when he or she should seek out additional help and when you might have to intervene directly.

If you feel you have to intervene directly, it does not mean that you confront the child. It may not even mean that you confront or try to talk with the other child's parents (this is sometimes helpful but can also be unproductive or even counterproductive). At times, parents may want to involve the school staff (e.g., principal, school social worker, school psychologist), a pediatrician, a mental health professional in the community, or another individual who can offer guidance. If serious threats have been made, the police may have to be consulted as well.

Even if you think the message that upset your child is minor, it's important to acknowledge that what is seen as minor to you may not be seen the same way by your child. Supporting, understanding, and helping your child are key reactions that help kids feel cared about and protected. If your child feels overwhelmed even after you talk about ways to cope, it's time to seek professional help.

Being a Guardian Versus Being a Censor

Whether parents' monitoring of their child's computer use is censorship or guardianship is a matter of debate. Have you thought about your philosophy on this issue? It's important to take a few minutes to truly think about this so that your actions seem congruent with your beliefs. However, it can be helpful first to be aware of a few crucial topics when it comes to the risks and benefits of screening your child's access to the world of technology:

- Your child may intentionally or inadvertently stumble across a site that is sexually explicit or filled with significant violence or information that he is not old enough to understand or that may emotionally overwhelm or affect him. And you may not know about this exposure. If you do not know what he is viewing, it's more difficult to help him move past it.

- Sometimes parents periodically monitor what their child is doing on the computer (don't be afraid to look over your child's shoulder when he's on the computer researching things for school, playing computer games, etc.) but do not realize that quick pop-ups sometimes offer your child the chance to move to another site that you would not approve of.

- Your child may play video games that look okay according to the packaging but whose level of violence you would find surprising. Previewing games has often helped parents avoid having their children be exposed to age-inappropriate content. When children play online or download to their game consoles, you have to be even more vigilant because there is no packaging to see.

- Even when children are playing video games with their friends over the Internet, other "children" may ask to join in or be invited by one of the friends to join. You may have heard horror stories about adults pretending to be children and connecting with children on sites that children frequent to learn personal information about a child. To protect your children from people who prey on children, it's important to monitor their computer contacts continually and repeatedly discuss stranger danger and how devious some predators can be. You probably know that even e-mails that appear to come from someone you know may, in fact, be a scam and not from that person at all. This is another topic to review with your child because it can make your computer vulnerable to hackers.

- When discussing the topic of stranger danger, take a few moments to also discuss that there are many good people in the world though you are only focusing on the ones that may be predators. Emphasizing the positives about humanity can help keep children from mistrusting everyone and can foster a discussion on how to discriminate between the positive and the potentially dangerous people with whom they may interact.

- Children and tweens, not only teenagers, send photos of themselves to friends or others. If your child is sending messages or photos to one person, they can be passed to others until many recipients have gotten them. Children tend to think of texting or sending a photo as a personal connection with the other person. However, it's a permanent record, and once they send it, they lose control over where the item goes next and who sees it. Children sometimes send photos or texts they would never show or discuss face-to-face with another person. Somehow, the "protective distance" of the computer makes the unacceptable seem acceptable. This warrants repeated discussions as your child grows. Even adults need reminders about this topic!

Raising children has always been an interesting but challenging experience. Now, there is a new component to deal with. It can be complicated to raise children at this time in history when they have access to so much information and an almost instant ability to communicate over their electronic devices. Many children, tweens, and adolescents have minicomputers (e.g., smartphones) that give them the ability to access knowledge, be exposed to information (appropriate and inappropriate), and share this material with others almost instantly. There are things you can do to allow your child to have the benefits of technology and to reduce the risks.

Fostering Independence While Monitoring Computer Use

Many young children quickly understand how to use a cell phone or computer. They often equate this knowledge with the belief that they should not be supervised for what they are doing. As adults, we know that having the skill does not mean knowing how to use it wisely or safely. That's where parenting comes in. As you know, parenting isn't always easy. At times, when you are monitoring or restricting computer access, you may find your child is annoyed by or even resents your intrusion. The following are some tips on how to allow your children some independence yet continue to monitor their technology use:

- By setting up your computer in a public location in your home (essentially a computer usage area where all devices such as laptops or iPads can be used), your child won't necessarily question whether you trust her since it's just the designated family technology location.
- Set appropriate times when technology can be used and when you can monitor it. If the family rule is no texting or technology at the dinner table, let the rule apply to everyone (except, of course, if you have an emergency situation to deal with).
- Learn about parental controls. There are some wonderful apps and programs that allow you to block certain sites from your children and keep you informed of their computer usage.
- If you aren't sure how to set up parental controls, you can ask questions at the local computer store, ask the administrators at your child's school, or even ask questions at the local police department.
- Spend some time with your child discussing why you have parental controls and the legal ramifications of misuse of the computer, smartphone, and so forth. Highlight that your child also has to be responsible and accountable for his behavior online (e.g., cyberbullying).
- Pick times to have honest discussions about th sharing private information or photos that th to be public, stranger danger (predators), an

- Does your child need access to technology in the middle of the night? If not, why not leave smartphones and other devices in a public place in the home or your bedroom?

Balancing the "Internet World" With the "Real World"

There are numerous pros and cons to Internet use. How do you balance the "when," "where," and "how"? These are tricky questions, but there are several important points to consider when answering these questions for your family.

Many parents struggle to figure out when to allow their children to have cell phones, for instance. Some parents have a set age that applies to all children in the family. Many other parents have attended local workshops on the risks and benefits of giving children cell phones and the age that children in their community tend to get them. Either way, ask yourself why your child would benefit from having it now. If you don't have an answer, it may not be the right time, despite your child's pleas.

If your child ends up being the last in his grade to get a cell phone, it might create social ramifications. Whenever you do give your child a phone, be clear on the rules, the legal consequences of sharing inappropriate content or pictures, and the risk of being misunderstood or hurting others by comments when voice tone or facial expressions are not evident. There are numerous apps that could allow you to monitor usage, texts, and so forth. Whether you use these apps is a personal parenting decision.

As you read in earlier chapters, executive functioning skills are important as children get older and more independent. Therefore, if you decide to give your child a cell phone, you may also want to give her some control of monitoring her phone usage. This way, she begins to learn the skill of self-monitoring and, hopefully, can keep the usage within the allotted parameters. Cell phone use, as well as access to other technology, raises challenging questions for parents.

Mr. and Mrs. Spellman struggled with the issue of how technology should be used in their home. When their children became school-aged, the parents decided to set up two computers in the house, one in the kitchen, the other in the living room. They picked these spots so they could easily glance at what their children were seeing and doing online. Because the children grew up with this setup, they accepted it (sometimes reluctantly) and often self-monitored so their parents continued to allow them access to the computers.

When the children were old enough to get cell phones, Mr. and Mrs. Spellman connected their phone to their children's so that they received information on what their children were doing online. In addition, at mealtime and family time, all cell phones were placed in a basket. This way, neither children nor parents were tempted to glance at their phones. When the children sometimes complained about this rule, the parents calmly said, "The rules apply to all of us. We want time just with our family."

Mr. and Mrs. Spellman believed that restricting their children's use of social media would lead them to be disadvantaged by missing out on this means of common communication. However, they noticed that their 7-year-old son was becoming socially awkward at group gatherings until they increased his face-to-face play dates to give him the opportunity to socialize in the "real-world" arena.

In a conversational fashion, often during car rides or dinner, Mr. and Mrs. Spellman discussed important and pertinent topics with their children. Several of these topics were technology related, such as cyberbullying, stranger danger, how nothing is truly private on the Internet and how a brief moment of writing something negative can ruin a friendship or cause someone to feel embarrassed, hurt, or worse. Therefore, when the Spellman children had the opportunity to use computers at friends' homes, when no adult was monitoring them, they remembered their lessons and stayed away from these damaging pitfalls.

If you want to help your child figure out the when, where, and how of Internet use in your family, consider some of the methods the Spellmans used. Discussing the rationale behind your decisions can help children internalize this logic so they can, hopefully, use it to self-monitor when you are not nearby. How much you monitor your child's cell phone use (e.g., having his activities reported back to your phone) is a very personal parental decision. In addition, because computers seem to be here to stay, we have to guide children toward a healthy balance between using technology and spending time without their devices.

WHAT TO DO WHEN THE LIGHTS GO OUT

As your children mature, it's not only helpful for them to be able to use technology but also to have the skills to socialize, enjoy life, and fill their time with creative and fun experiences that require no electricity or computers. Many parents have reported that when technology is not available at all, such as during a blackout, they find it rewarding to have everyone available to participate in family activities. There are also times when parents have encouraged family members to move away from computer time and focus more on other things.

There are numerous skills children can develop in the "old-fashioned" way. The following are just a few activities you can help your child enjoy when technology is not being used:

- Siblings of different ages focus on social media or being with same-age friends. When the lights go out (or your family goes away on a trip or camping), it is a great opportunity for siblings to do things together and have fun with one another.

- Children can play games such as hide-and-go-seek, play on the playground, engage in physical games, learn board games, and so forth. Many of these activities can be played by children of different ages, and even adults can participate and enjoy them!
- Face-to-face conversation helps children focus on the many bits of information available, including voice intonations, facial expressions, humor, and dialogues.
- This time allows your child to share more than she might if she felt the emotional pull to get onto the computer.
- This time allows children to have quiet "me time" when they find ways to create new games or art projects, learn how to entertain themselves, and do not worry about getting onto a social media site or playing a video game.

You may wonder how to achieve these goals. The following are some tips:

- Over dinner or at another time when your family is all together, have everyone join in creating a list of what games or activities they might want to try when computers are not available. Then, when the lights go out, you have the necessary items, and everyone can play these games together (even by candlelight or flashlight), have a group scavenger hunt, try a new skill (e.g., painting with watercolors), or try a fun athletic experience together.
- Have activities ready to use at home (e.g., jigsaw puzzle, baking ingredients) or places to go to enjoy activities in the community (e.g., playground). This can be helpful so that when the time allows, you already have a plan.
- Many families have found that it's a good idea to turn off all technology at times each week so that family members can stay connected and other activities can be shared.

- Sometimes face-to-face conversation happens naturally, but sometimes it may be awkward when a child is quiet or less verbal. For these children, consider picking a fun, nonthreatening topic to begin the conversation when the computers are turned off (e.g., "What would you say if your favorite TV star were here for dinner?" "If you had the power to make the world better in one way, what would you do?").

- Before cell phones were available, traveling in the car provided a great opportunity for conversation with children, who were a captive audience. Today, when driving, there may be times when a cell phone, movie, or another form of distraction is okay to use, but at other times you can call the car ride a "technology-free" zone. At these times, you could try an old game of finding license plates from the most states.

- If your child is not sure how to fill time when no friends are around, no sibling is available to play with, and no technology is accessible, introduce him to the world of creative play.

The world of play, without computers, can be amazing, special, relaxing, and exciting all at the same time. For instance, for Kimberly's third birthday, her aunt wrapped a huge, empty box and gave it to her. When she opened it and everyone saw it was empty, the adults thought her aunt had forgotten the gift. However, over time, Kimberly turned this box into a table, a hideaway, a stove, a store counter, and several other items. Her aunt informed her parents that the true gift was the opportunity to use her imagination.

Blocks, LEGOs, dolls, and other toys that have stood the test of time all allow a child to entertain himself and use imagination and creativity. You can encourage this play by sometimes sitting with your child and asking what he is doing and how he can include you in that activity.

SUMMARY

Technology offers many advantages, such as easy access to information, ease of communication, and entertainment. It also presents risks to children when they play certain video games, stumble across inappropriate sites, interact with strangers over the Internet, or misuse their social media (intentionally or innocently).

Technology also presents parents with special challenges when they try to supervise their children's use of their cell phone, iPad, computer, and so forth. In this chapter, both the advantages and disadvantages of children accessing these devices were explored in detail. In the upcoming chapter, we discuss significant life stressors that can act as triggers for parents to become overprotective and lessen their children's ability to be independent. We show you ways to help children survive and eventually thrive, even when confronted with these challenges.

CHAPTER 9

RAISING INDEPENDENT CHILDREN IN SPECIAL CIRCUMSTANCES

Parents often try to protect their children from disappointments, stress, and difficulties in life. As you read in Chapter 5, however, some frustration helps children build coping skills and confidence so they can manage difficulties and challenges as they grow into independent adults.

There are times when children are faced with adverse situations, often beyond their control, such as the loss of a loved one. When these circumstances arise, children may feel overwhelmed or confused and may require special care from parents so they can continue to thrive. Behavioral, emotional, or learning challenges can also have a significant impact on children. It's important to remember, however, that this does not necessarily mean that these individuals will have difficulty as grown-ups. When you're parenting during an exceptional time—if a family member has received a serious medical diagnosis, for example—you may be tempted to overcompensate for any stress the situation causes your child. Of course, giving your child a little extra TLC (tender loving care) during this time is simply showing love, support, and understanding. If your family is facing a challenging time, it's also helpful to remember that even the most difficult circumstances can allow for children to model from your coping strategies and your discussions about how to deal with life's stresses. This experience, then, can be one that helps them cope with other difficulties when they become independent adults.

Before reading further in this chapter, take a minute to reflect on whether your child has experienced special circumstances (e.g., loss, attention-deficit/hyperactivity disorder, shyness, anxiety, divorce) and, if so, how comfortable you have been with guiding her without being overprotecting.

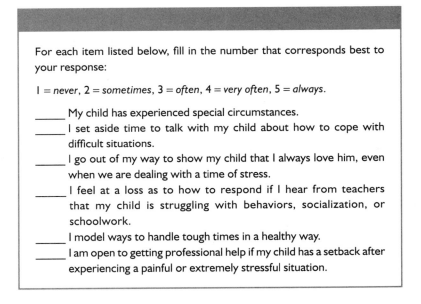

For each item listed below, fill in the number that corresponds best to your response:

1 = *never*, 2 = *sometimes*, 3 = *often*, 4 = *very often*, 5 = *always*.

_____ My child has experienced special circumstances.

_____ I set aside time to talk with my child about how to cope with difficult situations.

_____ I go out of my way to show my child that I always love him, even when we are dealing with a time of stress.

_____ I feel at a loss as to how to respond if I hear from teachers that my child is struggling with behaviors, socialization, or schoolwork.

_____ I model ways to handle tough times in a healthy way.

_____ I am open to getting professional help if my child has a setback after experiencing a painful or extremely stressful situation.

In this chapter, you will read about specific circumstances some children experience and how you can support and guide them through these adverse times. The coping strategies you teach them today can often be applied to difficult situations in the future when they are adults.

SPECIAL LIFE CIRCUMSTANCES AND HEALTHY COPING

There are children and even young adults who become anxious or even emotionally paralyzed by their first experience with significant stress. When children and teenagers do not have the opportunity to learn that they can handle difficult situations on their own, they may not develop a toolbox of coping strategies for these situations as they grow up. In the following sections, we offer ideas for teaching these strategies in specific situations.

Loss of a Loved One

Many children experience loss over the course of their childhood. Some children first experience death when a pet dies. Others have to deal with the loss of a grandparent or extended family member. Sometimes a parent or sibling dies, often creating a multitude of feelings and changes for all the surviving family members. When a member of the household dies, children have to deal not only with grief but also a change in the daily routine and family dynamics.

Death is a concept that means different things depending on your child's age. A young child of 3 may feel death is temporary and then grieve the same loss again when time has passed and he realizes that the loved one is not returning. In this second time of grieving, it is equally important to validate and support your child as he tries to grasp the permanence of the situation. A teenager who experiences loss for the first time may have previously felt invulnerable, is now suddenly aware that life is a temporary situation, and can regress (act younger) because of the recognition that he is vulnerable and mortal.

Children often wish or believe that their parents are capable of fixing everything if they try. Therefore, if a loved one dies, some children and even teenagers become angry and defiant as a way to express their disappointment and fear at your inability to make the world right for them.

There is no one right way for children to respond, but there are ways you can help your child cope with these painful experiences. When a distant relative or neighbor dies, it is a good time to mention loss and model how to deal with it. If a pet dies, it is often an emotional time for a child as well as parents and not to be minimized. It is an appropriate time to start teaching rituals and other coping techniques.

The following are some tips on helping your child deal with loss:

- Accept any feelings he expresses as being acceptable and valid, even if you think the thoughts are illogical.
- A child who is angry at the deceased and a child who is sad are both children whose feelings have to be acknowledged as justified. Children can often get upset with the deceased for abandoning them (not always, but especially when a loved one had engaged in an action that may have hastened the death, such as smoking).
- Try to explain the cause of death in a way that won't make children worry that they are also likely to die soon. Even if the loss is of a sibling, mention how rare it is for a child to die, but then explain the cause in language your child can understand.
- In the unlikely event that the sibling died from suicide, you may want to focus more on the depression or other underlying issues that led to the behavior, especially if the surviving sibling is young.
- If you find yourself crying, it's important to let your child know that this is okay and even a healthy reaction to loss. However, some children and even teenagers may feel you are overwhelmed and unable to parent them in your time of grief. Therefore, even when crying, you should sometimes remind your child that you are still capable of being there to support her.

- Family rituals for dealing with loss often allow children to know what to do at this difficult time. These rituals help adults too. At funerals, wakes, shiva visits, or other family gatherings, saying kind words, looking at pictures, and telling stories about the deceased can all provide children with a sense of comfort as they learn more about what to expect and ways to react.
- Religious beliefs and traditions of your family, including prayers and ceremonies, can give your child a sense of comfort because he knows what religious rituals will occur when a person dies.
- Many religious beliefs about what happens after death can provide your child with another sense of comfort that the deceased is not entirely gone (if life after death is, in fact, a belief that you hold).
- There is no definitive right or wrong about whether your child should attend a funeral, wake, shiva, or other ritualized ceremony or engage in grieving customs. This should be determined on a child-by-child basis. You can seek the guidance of a religious leader or mental health counselor to determine whether your child should attend some of these rituals, not attend but be told about them, or be shielded from them entirely.
- If your child is not made aware of the fact that a person has died, he may feel the person is purposely rejecting or abandoning him. Therefore, it's helpful to explain that the person can no longer be physically present.

Of course, even after reading these tips, it's not an easy task to help your child to navigate his way through understanding death and enjoying life without the loved one. With your help, and sticking to routines your child is accustomed to, many children and teenagers learn to cope with the changes. Children may always feel the loss of an important person, such as a parent, but they can learn to move forward and eventually continue to thrive.

There are times when children get stuck in their grief and struggle to engage in the activities of the living. This is not unusual for a few weeks after a loss. Some children even become school phobic because they fear you may die if they are not watching you. They may fear going to sleep because they fear they might not wake up. If you notice your child is struggling with fears of death or showing anxiety even after the first few weeks of grieving, a child psychologist or social worker may be able to offer some tips on helping your child overcome these fears.

If your child continues to feel sad, anxious, or angry for many weeks and is not returning to some sense of her former schedule, it can be a sign of depression or complicated bereavement rather than healthy grieving. If the intensity of your child's sadness and the length of time of the grieving affects her ability to function in her daily life and no healing has started, your child may be depressed. Depression can prevent your child from moving through the stages of grieving (as identified by researcher Elizabeth Kübler Ross; see the Suggested Readings list for more information).

Children can talk about death and loss for years, expressing sadness as they move through different developmental stages. For instance, Craig lost his father at the age of 7. After his initial grieving, he returned to his social, athletic, and school life. However, his mother recalled that at age 11, right before his elementary school graduation, Craig became sullen about his father not being present for this ceremony. Years later, when he graduated from high school and later married, he again felt a strong wave of sadness. Wishing for the deceased to have a physical presence in one's life is a normal reaction, especially during significant events, such as holidays and birthdays.

If you are concerned about whether your child is grieving in a healthy fashion or getting "stuck" in depression or a complicated bereavement, it's "better to be safe than sorry." As mentioned earlier in regard to anxiety, consult a mental health professional if you think your child needs some coping tools to regain the focus on life and deal with feelings of sadness and thoughts about the loss.

Separation and Divorce

Over the years, we have learned that there are a variety of ways that separated or divorced parents can reduce the trauma to their children. However, even with the same parental actions, some children have more difficulty adjusting to divorce than others.

Many parents seeking a divorce feel some relief when the spouse is no longer living with them and even more relief when the divorce is finalized. However, children report that even at these times, there can be a tug-of-war involving the children. Because many children want to be loyal to both parents and see themselves as connected to them, one parent's disparaging comments about the other can have the unintended consequence of hurting the children and their self-esteem. For instance, 12-year-old Malcolm commented to his therapist, "I'm part of my mom and my dad. When my dad tells me how awful my mom is, I feel like he's hating part of who I am. Why does he do that?"

Do you remember the biblical story of Solomon? As a judge, he was confronted by two women arguing over who was the mother of a child. Solomon suggested that they cut the baby in half so that both women had a piece of the child. When one woman said, "No! Give it to her (as she pointed to the other woman)," Solomon knew she was the real mother because she put the needs of the baby ahead of her own. Clearly, we never want anyone to suggest cutting up or harming a baby, but it is a story with the profound message that children need protection, and their needs must come before the desires or wants of the parents (e.g., when involved in hostile divorce procedures). Sometimes this is easier to think and believe than to do.

Divorce can raise parental feelings of wanting to be seen as the favored parent and to show children the flaws of the other. It can be hard to hold back from sharing a negative reality with your child. If you are concerned about your child's safety, you should immediately seek legal or mental health counseling on how to protect him. Otherwise, you can confirm to your child that the other parent isn't your friend right now but you will try to work on coparenting, when possible.

The following are some tips for helping your child adjust to divorce:

- When parental conflicts begin, there may be times when children are asked to take sides or speak for one parent to the other. They may even get less attention because the conflict is taking a lot of the energy from the parents. When parents are sensitive to these issues, it can make the trauma of parental disagreements somewhat less painful for children.

- Divorce doesn't happen in a day, so the consideration for children should begin even before divorce procedures start. If yelling, fighting, or disagreements were present before the divorce, it probably affected your child. Children can move forward, but it can help if both parents agree that they will work together to make the children's environment more harmonious and less conflictual.

- It can also be helpful for both parents to tell their children that the relationship wasn't all negative because they came from it. This validates that they are valued.

- Visitation schedules should put children first so that they don't miss activities, feel pushed and pulled, or feel that their schedules are unpredictable.

- Even when visitation schedules seem fair in regard to the time children are in each parent's household, its impact on your child's daily life should also be considered (e.g., school, friends, sports, activities).
- Children may fear being abandoned by the noncustodial parent, requiring both the custodial and noncustodial parent to convey the same message that both parents will continue to raise them (if this is the actual arrangement).
- Many schools will send information and announcements to both parents unless there is a legal reason not to. Speak with your child's principal to determine whether your child's school does this.
- Both parents (together or separately) should try to stay in touch with those who also guide their children (e.g., classroom teacher) and show interest in activities (e.g., Little League games, school concerts).

If parents settle into a coparenting relationship without arguments, the grown-ups may feel more comfortable, but children may still need more time and support to accept and adjust to this major change in their lives. For the long term, modeling that both parents can work together for the sake of the children can lead your child to develop coping strategies for working through problems she may have with others when she is older (e.g., coworkers, neighbors, teachers).

Some children prefer arguments to divorce, whereas others welcome the end of the warring household. Listening to and respecting their views and feelings can have a big impact. Therefore, keeping an open line of communication with your child, so he can honestly express his reaction to the changes in the family life, is extremely important. This way you can know what he feels, thinks, and wants and when and if he needs some professional intervention to help in the adjustment process.

Blended Families

If you are at a point in your life when you want to date others, keep in mind that your child may not agree on the time frame or like the idea of you dating. If you put your child's needs first and feel you also have time to focus on your personal life, dating may be the next step for you. If you do date, you don't have to ask permission, but you also don't have to expose your child to everyone you date. This could lead to anger, an attachment to someone who is only going to be in your life briefly, and lots of adjustments as you engage in new relationships.

Children like to know what parents are doing, so you can let them know (depending on their ages) that you are dating and will introduce them if the relationship seems like it's getting serious. Before you end up living with a new partner, husband, or wife, give your child time to get to know the person, share experiences that can bond them, and help her see that even with the new person around you, she is the priority.

Each situation is different with blended families. Are there going to be stepsiblings? If so, are they close in age, or is there a significant age difference? Will you move into a new home or keep the house that your "ex" shared with you? Every choice and thought helps you consider how to support and protect your child's feelings. The Mayo Clinic offers tips you might consider when blending families (see Suggested Readings).

The following are some additional things to think about:

- If you will have stepchildren, how will you help them to feel cared about without making your child feel neglected, overlooked, or jealous?
- If the new members of the blended family have traditions that are different from yours, how will you address this so

all individuals feel their backgrounds are acknowledged and respected?

- Will your child and a stepchild share a room? What are the pros and cons of these particular children living so close together? How will they plan to decorate the room and decide whose items go where?
- How can you work to still coparent with your child's other parent while now also including your new partner in your child's life?
- Before living together, discuss with your new partner his or her philosophy on raising children and how he or she will assume a role in the life of your child.

Blended families can be viewed as positive in that they can provide your child a larger support system and more people to learn from and share experiences with. However, if the other parent is uncomfortable with the new arrangement and shares his or her feelings with your child, it can create a loyalty issue for your child. In addition, if a child is resistant to the creation of this blended family, it's not a time to demand or criticize. Listening, reflecting on your child's feelings, explaining why the situation is occurring, and spending one-on-one time showing your child that your relationship with him is not changing despite the new love in your life may all be helpful.

If your child continues to be uncomfortable, you can seek professional guidance on how everyone in your blended family can find their special role and lead to your child having a better outlook and coping strategy. However, listen to your child carefully. Sometimes a child has valid complaints or concerns that warrant your taking action to support her and change the situation. In addition, if your blended family involves your entering into a same-sex relationship with your partner or a relationship with a person of a different ethnic, racial, or religious background, it may or may not be an issue for your child, but openly discussing it can show your child that it's okay to come to you and share her feelings on these topics, should she have any to explore.

WHEN YOUR CHILD HAS A PERSONAL CHALLENGE

Unfortunately, in one book, we can't focus on every possible challenge that may face your child. However, we will discuss several common issues including attention-deficit/hyperactivity disorder, learning disabilities, learning differences, physical challenges, anxiety, and shyness.

Attention-Deficit/Hyperactivity Disorder

Attention-deficit/hyperactivity disorder or ADHD is diagnosed when a child or adult has significant difficulty with paying attention or being overactive and/or impulsive or has both of these symptom clusters. Although making the diagnosis is a bit more complicated than this, these symptoms are the major areas considered. A child can have the diagnosis without hyperactivity but with inattention or be diagnosed with hyperactivity without inattention.

Sometimes parents feel overwhelmed when a child shows ADHD symptoms and may even wonder about their parenting skills and whether their child is simply being oppositional or unwilling to please. In fact, ADHD is generally thought to be a neurobiological condition, not a purposeful decision to act out or avoid focusing. Luckily, there are many strategies to support children with ADHD. The book *Learning to Slow Down and Pay Attention* (see the Suggested Readings list) explores a variety of intervention tools children can read about and implement, sometimes with adult support.

If you suspect your child has ADHD, it's worth pursuing further information and/or consulting a psychiatrist, neurologist, or psychologist so that you know more about what is happening with him or her. For instance, at the age of 8, Nicholas was exhausting his mother. Mrs. Collins confided in the pediatrician,

> Nicholas is so stubborn. He wants everything his way. It takes me hours every night to get him to sit down to do his homework. He also doesn't think. He jumps on furniture, runs into the street without looking both ways, and does other reckless things. He doesn't listen to my husband or to me. His teachers also say he is constantly moving around the classroom, losing his books and papers, and calling out. The teacher and I tried stickers to motivate Nicholas, and he seemed to want them, but he keeps doing all these behaviors. I need help.

The pediatrician wrote down the symptoms Mrs. Collins described, then talked about possible causes. For Nicholas, these included

- Nicholas reacting to his father's much longer work hours in his new job;
- Nicholas having a learning difficulty causing him to feel frustrated and agitated;
- the birth of his sister 3 years earlier, at which time Mrs. Collins began to feel concerned about his impulsivity and behavior difficulties;
- medical issues, such as hormonal concerns (e.g., thyroid, pituitary, adrenal);
- ADHD; and
- a stress that Nicholas may be experiencing that his mother does not know about or may not think is truly stressful.

The pediatrician carefully explored each of these topics with Mrs. Collins. The first and third potential causes were ruled out because Nicholas had exhibited the symptoms since age 3, although his mother hadn't felt concerned then because he was an only child at that point and she had the energy to support him despite his difficulties. After receiving blood work results on Nicholas, the pediatrician ruled out hormonal causes as well.

The pediatrician sent out some behavior rating forms to teachers and asked them to report on Nicholas's rate of learning new skills when he was focused and calm. The teachers sent these forms back, noting that Nicholas was a quick learner and acquired and retained information easily. However, they rated him high on impulsivity, restlessness, and significant inattention.

After receiving all this information, the pediatrician suggested that Mrs. Collins take Nicholas to a child psychiatrist to determine whether he had ADHD and whether medication might be useful. Mrs. Collins was concerned about medication but did go to the psychiatrist. After reviewing the findings from the pediatrician and also determining that Nicholas's difficulties were not due to excessive anxiety, panic, or agitated depression, the psychiatrist diagnosed Nicholas with ADHD. When Mrs. Collins heard about the medication options and the side effects, she hesitantly agreed to let him try it.

Within a few days, Nicholas showed an increased ability to sit, attend, and be cooperative. Of course, his medication was not the only thing necessary to help him. He also started in counseling, and his mother and father learned some tools to help them support their enthusiastic, sometimes-challenging son.

If you have a child with ADHD, you can use the following tips to help you focus on helping that child become a confident, independent adult:

- Judicious use of medication, if indicated, does not reflect your failure to raise your child to understand societal rules. It's not about your child not wanting to do the right thing and needing "to be drugged," it's about helping a child with a neurobiological condition get the help you may more comfortably give a child with another condition (e.g., insulin for a child with diabetes).

- The teacher or a counselor can probably guide you in developing a positive behavior modification plan to reward your child for adaptive behaviors.

- Be a detective—if your child is calmer after running around, get her involved in sports for which impulsivity isn't an issue (e.g., tennis, running). If your child is calmer after resting, you may want to investigate some meditation or mindfulness activities.

- Brainstorm with the teacher some accommodations or modifications that might be appropriate for your child (e.g., running errands, using a desk bike in class, being assigned fewer homework problems to do nightly).

- Spend time reviewing information from other chapters in this book with your child with ADHD. Developing frustration tolerance, executive functioning skills, and so forth, are important for all children, but those with ADHD may have to review these topics more frequently. It can be helpful if you spend time discussing how to apply this knowledge to their daily lives.

- If your child continues to struggle with schoolwork despite interventions, you can talk to the school psychologist about whether your child is eligible for a 504 accommodation plan. This plan is part of the Americans With Disabilities Act and helps children with significant life challenges have an equal chance to succeed in school.

Finally, any child who lacks self-confidence is a child who is more vulnerable. Therefore, if children with ADHD feel inferior, frustrated with their actions, confused about why it's hard for them to contain their impulses or why they can't focus on their work as well as their peers, these are important topics to explore. It can be helpful to remind your child that ADHD symptoms are not who he is, just something he needs to work around. Spend some time sharing your perception of who your child truly is—his strengths and interests, and why you love your child! Such positive affirmations can go a long way to helping children feel better about themselves.

Learning Disabilities, Learning Differences, and Physical Challenges

Any struggle can affect children's sense of competence and, therefore, their self-confidence about being able to deal with the world. However, when these same children learn to be resilient and realize their challenges do not entirely define them, it can lead to coping strategies that can benefit them for a lifetime.

School is often the first challenge children face outside the home. If students find that classmates have an easier time picking up new concepts, it can lead to frustration and doubts about their own academic capabilities. Learning disabilities (e.g., significant difficulty learning in the traditional way teachers present lessons), learning differences (e.g., preference for a different way of being taught based on learning style), or physical disabilities (e.g., struggles with significantly moving about or playing recess games) can all affect children.

When Sasha was 9 years old, she disliked school, frequently "forgot" to do her homework, and often feigned illness to stay home. Her parents felt she was smart because she shared many creative ideas and was able to do puzzles, draw, and even play educational games on the computer at the age of 3. By fourth grade, however,

Sasha's parents and teacher noticed she consistently struggled with written language and auditory learning in school. Eventually, Sasha was tested and found to have a language-based learning disability that significantly affected her academic performance. Despite the extra help, these skills remained areas of relative weakness.

As Sasha got older, she found she loved and was quite talented at graphic design. She decided to volunteer, intern, and eventually learn how to be a graphic designer by working in the industry rather than by going to college. Her parents were concerned about their daughter not getting a college education, and they talked with the school's guidance counselor about their concerns. The guidance counselor told them that there are many roads to success and that Sasha was a bright, talented young woman who could find success by taking any of them, not just the one that led to college. College was an option for her if the path that presently interested her did not lead to the goal she sought.

Sasha eventually worked as a graphic designer and later received accolades for her work. Having a learning disability that affected her academic performance in school did not stop her, nor did it hinder her potential for success. She had many of the coping strategies reviewed in earlier chapters, which helped her to work past her challenges and focus on her strengths. Later on, Sasha was curious about college and decided to take some night classes. She enjoyed the experience, took the classes at a pace that was comfortable for her, and eventually felt pride in having reached a new goal: attaining a college diploma.

If you suspect your child has school-related difficulties in functioning, it can be helpful to do the following:

- Consult the classroom teacher to see whether your perceptions are accurate or whether your child is just developing at a different but still typical rate.

- If your child's teacher suspects your child is having difficulties, ask what can and should be done, such as getting extra help, encouragement, and incentives for taking risks to try.
- You or your child's teacher may be able to determine (sometimes simply by watching) how your child learns best. For instance, does he like to see things, hear things, or touch things to learn most comfortably? Once this is known, your child can be supported in ways that fit his learning preference.
- If you suspect your child has a physical difficulty (e.g., gross motor movements, fine-motor coordination, vision, hearing), consult a pediatrician who can recommend specific testing. Sometimes there is a simple remedy, such as having your child wear glasses or a hearing aid.
- If you or your child's teacher suspects your child has a learning disability or a physical difficulty that affects her in school, testing can be helpful in determining your child's strengths and challenges and in figuring out some recommendations.

The following are a few things you can do at home:

- Listen to your child's concerns and fears about her abilities, and reflect that you heard them by summarizing what she said.
- Encourage your child to try new tasks and reinforce his efforts, but set realistic expectations commensurate with his current abilities.
- Remind your child about what makes her unique and special and what her strengths and talents are.
- Support your child in using positive self-talk and knowing when to ask for help.
- Remind yourself that even children who have weaknesses can have major strengths that lead to major success in life!

Diversity is necessary for a well-functioning community. Imagine a world in which everyone went to college and became doctors, lawyers, accountants, and so forth. It's important, and essential, to have painters, plumbers, electricians, mechanics, and others in a society. Therefore, as your child goes through school, monitor areas of strength as well as challenges so that the best path for him can be determined as the high school years approach. This does not, in any way, imply that children with learning disabilities can't become professionals. There are a multitude of factors that make a particular job a good fit for a particular person. Clearly, your child will also have a say in what he wants to pursue, but your input can be invaluable.

Anxiety and Shyness

Some infants appear to be social, outgoing, and comfortable around others, whereas some are reserved, anxious, and shy. There are children who once seemed to be outgoing but then become quieter as they go through developmental stages or life experiences. Of course, there are children who are initially shy or anxious and gradually become more outgoing.

If you notice that your child is reserved, it may not be anything to be concerned about, especially if she has the language skills and the ability to communicate clearly when she has something to say. Being reserved or quiet might mean your child is an observer who takes time to reflect before commenting. A quiet child may appear shy, but this may not be the case. Some quiet children are comfortable speaking up when they have something to say but otherwise prefer to remain quiet and listen. There are many adults who have benefitted from having this personality style. However, other children experience anxiety and shyness and are uncomfortable in a variety of circumstances because of apprehension that they won't be liked, worry that what they say will be met with disapproval, or fear that they won't be able to master a situation.

If your child appears to be anxious or shy with peers, you can try the following:

- Figure out whether it's truly anxiety and shyness or simply that your child is being reserved.
- Speak with the teacher to see how your child interacts when you are not present. Sometimes a quiet, anxious child becomes more outgoing when her parent is not around.
- Ask the teacher for suggestions to help your child overcome anxiety and feel more comfortable with peers.
- If your child suddenly changes from being outgoing and comfortable with others to being anxious and withdrawn, take time to explore whether some event caused him to change. If so, explore the situation and figure out whether an intervention is needed.
- If your child is shy, peers may misinterpret this as a lack of interest in them (when teenagers are shy, their classmates might even think they are snobbish). Therefore, it can be useful to have a discussion with your child about how to let others know she is interested in a friendship, despite the shyness.
- Even shy children can practice and learn key responses such as eye contact, smiling, and saying something to connect with peers (e.g., "What are you doing this weekend?") so that the other children know your child is interested in them.
- Try to set up a variety of play dates with peers, so your child can have one-on-one time with others who share common interests (e.g., playing appropriate computer games, going to an art workshop in your community). Scheduling short, successful, and structured play dates is often a good way for shy children to feel more comfortable expanding their social circle.

If your child remains socially anxious and shy, and you do not see a gradual change, it may be time to seek the support of a mental health professional who can guide you and help your child to feel more comfortable. A child who struggles with anxiety and shyness throughout childhood is a child who may not fully engage in all the enjoyment of childhood activities and new experiences and who may hesitate to embrace increasing levels of independence.

SQUEAKY WHEELS

Have you ever heard the expression "A squeaky wheel gets the grease"? This phrase simply means that the squeaky wheel gets more attention than the non-squeaky wheel. The same pattern is noticed with children: A child who is a squeaky wheel is a child who tends to get more attention.

For instance, a child who has a physical disability, an emotional difficulty, or a highly reactive personality may be referred to as a "high-maintenance" child. You may have to spend a significant amount of time supporting these children, but you should also set aside some time when things are going well to reinforce their adaptive, independent behaviors.

You probably realize that you not only have to monitor these children but also consider the impact your attention to them has on siblings. You can schedule special times with quieter children so they get an equal amount of your attention and don't end up resenting their sibling or your time with that sibling—and so they don't learn that they have to be a squeaky wheel to get your attention.

SUMMARY

In this chapter, some powerful life stressors were explored, such as loss, divorce, and individual challenges (e.g., ADHD, learning disabilities, physical challenges, shyness). If your child experiences such situations, it's important to think about his circumstances and needs. You can then use the challenge as a time for "teachable moments" to build coping strategies and resilience rather than allowing it to affect your child's confidence and willingness to pursue new experiences and goals.

If your child is overwhelmed by a particular situation (e.g., school, parties, talking with others) and your support has not decreased symptoms, it can be helpful to ask the teacher or school psychologist for tips. If the situation does not improve after that, it may be time to seek help from a mental health professional in your community.

CONCLUSION

After reading this book and implementing the various strategies in it, can you now guarantee that your child will grow up to be a well-balanced, self-confident, and independent adult? Unfortunately, the answer is NO! There are many outside influences—peer groups, siblings, teachers, environmental factors, world events, medical issues— that also affect your child's growth and development, positively or negatively.

Consider the example of Allie, who had a close relationship with her parents, siblings, and extended family members. She learned many things from her relatives but developed her love of science after working on a research paper in high school with her science teacher. She learned a lot from her coach about sportsmanship while playing lacrosse. Her parents were relieved to realize they didn't have to become experts on every topic or be the sole mentors for Allie.

Of course, there are influences in your child's world that may not be beneficial, or maybe even harmful. For instance, your child may be influenced by peer pressure to try alcohol or drugs, cut school, or engage in bullying behaviors. However, hopefully your strong relationship with your child will allow him or her to find a way to reject these influences.

As Allie's parents learned, parents are not alone in striving to reach the goal of teaching their children everything they need for their future. If you have a trusting relationship and open communication with your child, you can guide her to include other appropriate, healthy role models in her world. In addition, if your child knows your guidance is logical and intended to support her, she may be more likely to accept rather than rebel against other "authority figures" who offer sound advice. Peers can also offer positive influences and expose your child to new experiences and learning.

If you put in the effort day after day and year after year (and it is an effort!) to help your child be confident, develop executive functioning skills, make independent and healthy decisions, self-monitor, tolerate frustrations, be socially comfortable, use technology wisely, and overcome adversity, your child will have a better chance of becoming a healthy, independent adult. If you have a close relationship with your child and have taught her these lessons, you will more likely have a child who is better prepared to face life's challenges independently, yet know when to ask for guidance.

KEY CONVERSATIONS TO BOOST YOUR CHILD'S INDEPENDENCE

Throughout this book, many topics have been explored, but there are some key points to remember. For instance, when talking with your child, try to

- explain, not criticize;
- discuss, not lecture;

- share ideas and your reasons for your decisions;
- take the time to value the ideas and opinions of your child;
- remind yourself that sometimes your child may seem stubborn when he sticks to something that you don't agree with, but appears to be persevering when he sticks to things you do agree with. Therefore, help your child to persevere, realize that sometimes his desire cannot be attained, and to realize when compromise or negotiation is needed;
- share stories from your life about when you had to abandon or change your goal and what steps you took to negotiate or compromise;
- rather than argue about specific words or behaviors you don't like, tell your child that being rude or disrespectful isn't the most effective way to have his message heard; and
- let him take more initiative in looking at the pros and cons of decisions so that the decision-making skills are internalized and not always dependent on your presence.

INCIDENTAL AND ACCIDENTAL MESSAGES

Whether your children admit it or not, a parent generally has a profound impact on them. Praise from a parent can be a powerful, wonderful experience, even when your child does not appear to be listening or reacting to it. Criticism and disapproval may have a detrimental effect and reduce a child's self-confidence, even when your child seems to shrug off your comments.

Well-intentioned parents like you don't set out to disapprove of or criticize their children. Sometimes it almost seems automatic to criticize a child's "silly," "ridiculous," "poorly thought-out," or "impulsive" ideas and behavior. One of the hardest parts of parenting is to use each misstep (your child's or your own!) as a learning opportunity. Perhaps it would be helpful to remember the adage "You can catch more flies with honey than with vinegar" and support your child's efforts while trying to help him or her become more self-reflective and not repeat mistakes.

Even when you work hard to be supportive and encouraging, you may not realize how attuned children are to your facial expressions, body language, and voice intonations. Although we teach children to accept that they are not perfect, we hope you are also kind to yourself when you are not perfect—it is important to be self-aware, model self-acceptance, and reflect on the messages you share every day.

The following are some messages children picked up that surprised their parents:

- When Luke wasn't picked for the varsity soccer team, he quickly accepted joining the junior varsity team. When his parents became upset and his father angrily said that the coach made a mistake in not selecting their son for the varsity team, Luke realized how important it had been to his parents, and he felt he let them down. His parents thought they were supporting him.

- Rachel's friends kept trying to get her to experiment with ice cream flavors other than the vanilla she always ordered. Rachel always made a face and said, "My family only eats vanilla ice cream." As it turns out, once when Rachel was getting ice cream with her family when she was younger, and they saw another customer ordering a different flavor ice cream, her mother quietly joked to Rachel, "Why would anybody order any other ice cream when vanilla is available?" Rachel didn't understand that her mother was kidding, took her mother's words at face value, and never questioned them as she got older.

Even teenagers like Luke and Rachel, who often challenge parental views and decisions, can be affected by your opinions and subtle messages. If you are just beginning to use the lessons from this book when your child is an adolescent, know that he can still be positively influenced by your input.

Parents who try to constantly educate their children on how to act, react, and work toward future goals are parents who are involved and working hard to raise their children. However, the incidental message to the growing child may be that the parents do not trust his or her judgment and attempts to make independent decisions. This topic has been explored repeatedly throughout this book but warrants being highlighted here.

If, for instance, your child wants to make her own decision when buying an age-appropriate book in the local bookstore or acceptable clothes that represent her taste (but wouldn't be something you would have bought for her), let her make more of these "safe" decisions. The consequences of these decisions are neither permanent nor life threatening.

If your child realizes she made wrong decisions and she says, "Mom, I hate this book" or "Why did I get this sweater? It's way too itchy for me," it is a great time to seize the moment to talk about how it's sometimes frustrating but valuable to take some time to think about the pros and cons before acting on wishes. A lesson learned firsthand is often a lesson remembered!

PASSING THE BATON

Your child is learning from you every moment, from birth onwards. Infants turn into toddlers, toddlers turn into children, children turn into tweens, tweens turn into teens, and before you know it, your infant is sitting across from you at the dinner table as a fully grown adult. One of the best gifts you can give your child is the belief you have confidence in the fact that your child is ready for the adult world and can make independent decisions.

Along the way, you or your child may stumble. You may wonder whether you can ever pass the baton to your child to handle the world and challenges without you. Despite the anxiety you might feel about passing the baton, it must eventually be passed. However, if your child has a close, respectful relationship with you, you will be more likely able to remain a "coach," available when your adult child has questions, needs guidance, or wants support. You may even be able to ask, "Do you want my opinion on this?" and get a response of "Yes!"

HARD WORK, FUN TIMES, REFLECTIONS

This book has focused on the key ingredients for raising a confident, independent adult. It's not easy work for parents. However, when your child is grown, you may look back on the years and wonder, "Where did the time go? It seemed to pass by so quickly." Therefore, even amidst all the hard work, take the time to enjoy the many positive experiences along the way!

Relish your child's smiles, schedule time to just play together doing something that you both enjoy or are experiencing for the first time, and take the time to admire how your child is growing, changing, and maturing. Soon your child will be a teenager, looking to spend more time with friends, so seize the moments you have now (and then) to create memories and have one-on-one times.

Wouldn't it be nice to have a crystal ball and see that your efforts will pay off and external factors won't significantly derail your child's healthy growth? Imagine gazing into your crystal ball and seeing yourself proudly sitting in the audience of your child's graduation from high school. Your son or daughter is now prepared to enter college or the workforce. You are filled with pride and nostalgia as well as amazement over the young adult you have raised. You hope that the lessons you taught your child over the last 17 to 18 years have been learned and absorbed.

You don't have a crystal ball to predict how your child will act or react today or tomorrow. Focus on today and hope that your child is learning the important lessons. If so, have confidence that your child is on the right track. Best of luck!

SUGGESTED READINGS

CHAPTER 1

Erikson, E. H. (1963). *Childhood and society* (2nd ed.). New York, NY: W. W. Norton & Company.

CHAPTER 2

Chapman, G., & Campbell, R. (2016). *The 5 love languages of children: The secret to loving children effectively.* Chicago, IL: Northfield.

CHAPTER 3

Pashler, H., McDaniel, M., Rohrer, D., & Bjork, R. (2008). Learning styles: Concepts and evidence. *Psychological Science in the Public Interest, 9,* 105–119. http://dx.doi.org/10.1111/j.1539-6053.2009.01038.x

Sternberg, R. J. (2015). Response to Pashler, Bjork, McDaniel, and Rohrer. *American Journal of Psychology, 128,* 125.

CHAPTER 4

The Colorado Education Initiative. (2014). *Grade 3–5 decision making.* Retrieved from http://www.coloradoedinitiative.org/wp-content/uploads/2014/10/Grade-3-5-Decision-Making.pdf

CHAPTER 5

Mischel, W. (2014). *The marshmallow test: Why self-control is the engine of success.* New York, NY: Little, Brown.

CHAPTER 6

Oswalt, A. (2010). *Moral development: Piaget's theory.* Retrieved from https://www.mentalhelp.net/articles/moral-development-piaget-s-theory/

CHAPTER 7

U.S. Department of Health and Human Services. *Stop bullying.* Retrieved from https://www.stopbullying.gov/

CHAPTER 8

HealthResearchFunding.org. (2015, July 21). *11 pros and cons of children using technology.* Retrieved from http://healthresearchfunding.org/11-pros-and-cons-of-children-using-technology/

CHAPTER 9

Gregory, C. (2017). *The five stages of grief: An examination of the Kubler-Ross model.* Retrieved from https://www.psycom.net/depression.central.grief.html

Mayo Clinic Staff. (2015). *Stepfamilies: How to help your child adjust.* Retrieved from http://www.mayoclinic.org/healthy-lifestyle/childrens-health/in-depth/stepfamilies/art-20047046

Nadeau, K. G., & Dixon, E. B. (2005). *Learning to slow down and pay attention: A book for kids about ADHD* (3rd ed.). Washington, DC: Magination Press.

INDEX

ADHD (attention-deficit/hyperactivity disorder), 220–224
Adolescence. *See also* Teenagers
early, 17–19
late, 19–22
and self-monitoring, 138
Adulthood, 22–23
Affirmative language, 52
After-school clubs, 71
Americans With Disabilities Act, 223
Anger, 122, 123, 166, 214
Anxiety
and confidence, 133
coping with, 227–229
and loss, 214
sharing your, 45–47
symptoms of, 12
Apologizing, 144
Assertiveness, 172, 177
Attention-deficit/hyperactivity disorder (ADHD), 220–224
Auditory learning style, 78
Autonomy. *See also* Independence
as cultural value, 4
encouragement of, 17

Bedtime, 70
Bedtime stories, 53–54
Behavior modification plans, 73, 137

Blended families, 218–220
Body language, 157–167
facial expressions, 160–161
on Internet, 187
and love, 52
and physical distance, 161–162
and physical presentation, 163–167
and verbal intonations, 157–158
Boredom, 158, 190
Bragging, 40, 41, 42
Brainstorming, 77, 95–97, 223
Bravado, 40–42, 129
Breathing techniques, 89, 110
Bullying
coping with, 171–178
cyber-, 131–132, 172, 187, 195–198
imbalance of power, 172
unintentional, 171
Bystanders, 175–176

Calming down, 88–90
Campbell, Ross, 52
Chapman, Gary, 52
Childproofing, 83
Choices, 17, 21, 31, 43, 66, 67, 82, 99, 104, 109, 126, 127, 129, 130, 147, 189
Clothing, 163–167

Communication skills, 21, 145,
  152–153. *See also* Social skills
Compliments, 42–44
Compromise, 21, 85–86
Confidence, 33–55
  bravado vs., 40–42
  and compliments, 42–44
  as element of independence, 12, 37
  and failure, 39–40
  and having different skills, 35–36
  lack of, 129, 133
  parenting methods for increasing,
    50–55
  parenting pitfalls with, 44–50
  putting in effort for helping child
    with, 232
  and social rejection, 170
  and success, 37–39
  of toddlers, 15
Conflict resolution, 85
Consequences, 98, 105–106,
  147–150
Cooperation, 106
Copyrights, 182
Corporal punishment, 146–147
Creativity, 12, 64
Critical thinking skills, 85
"Criticizing parent," 47–49, 233
"Critiquing parent," 47–49
Crying, 109, 120, 123, 145, 212
Curiosity, 77–78
Cyberbullying
  coping with, 172
  overview, 131–132
  and technology, 187, 195–198

Death, 211–215
Decision making, 81–99
  advice for helping your child with,
    97–99
  and brainstorming, 95–97
  in elementary school years, 84–89
  and frustration tolerance, 117–119
  and problem solving, 82–83, 85

in teenage years, 89–96
in toddler years, 83–84
Defensiveness, 144
Delayed gratification, 112–114
Dependency
  balance between independence and,
    15, 18
  outcomes of, 13
Depression, 212, 214, 222
Developmental stages, 14–23
Discomfort, 27, 43, 59, 102, 103, 109,
  119, 161, 162
Discussions, 89–91
Divergent thinking, 96
Divorce, 215–217
Dreams, 62
Dress, 130, 163–167

Early adolescence, 17–19
Early adulthood, 22–23
Effective parent, 103,116–117
Elementary school-aged children
  decision making by, 84–89
  and moderation, 136
Emotional pain, 114–116
Empathy, 90, 93
Ethnicity, 219–220
Executive functioning skills, 57–80
  and ADHD, 223
  challenges with development of, 59
  and curiosity, 77–78
  definitions of, 57
  flexible thinking for, 76
  and learning styles, 78–80
  life without, 59–61
  and organize, 57, 59, 61, 69, 74, 75,
    78, 109, 150, 182, 183
  and perseverance, 73–75
  prioritization and time management
    as, 69–71
  putting in effort for helping child
    with, 232
  and realistic vs. unrealistic goals,
    64–65

and self-monitoring, 138
and self-motivation, 71–73
short-term and long-term goals as
part of, 62–64, 68
and steps for guiding your child,
68–69
and steps in realistic goals, 65–68
and technology, 202–203

FaceTime, 181, 186
Facial expressions, 160–161, 187, 205
Failure, 39–40, 45, 223
Family rituals, 213
Fashion, 163–167
Feedback, 47–49
*The 5 Love Languages of Children:
The Secret to Loving Children
Effectively* (Chapman &
Campbell), 52
Flexible thinking, 39, 64, 76
Focusing preferences, 79
Friendships, 86
Frustration tolerance, 101–124
and child's age, 108–112
decision making around, 117–119
as different across children, 103–106
and immediate vs. delayed
gratification, 112–114
importance of, 102–103, 116–117
modeling of, 123
and protection against emotional
pain, 114–116
putting in effort for helping child
with, 232
and self-monitoring, 138
situations likely to provoke, 106–108
and specialness, 119–120
strategies for, 16
tips for responding to, 120–123

Games, 59, 66, 82, 88, 115, 129, 137,
159, 181, 184, 186, 188, 189,
190, 193, 194, 199, 205, 207,
217, 224, 228

Gifts, 52, 235
Goals
focusing on, 99
long-term, 62–64, 86
realistic vs. unrealistic goals, 64–65
short-term, 62–64, 68, 76, 86, 99
steps in realistic, 65–68
Google Docs, 181
Grammar check, 191
Grief, 211–215
Grooming, 163–167
Group projects, 181
Guidance, 23–24, 65–67
Guilt, 108, 117, 119, 123

Helicopter parenting, 28–29
Hemingway, Ernest, 52
Homework
consequences of neglecting, 98, 105
and executive functioning, 62, 68,
70, 71
helping out with, 54
independent starting of, 4
Humor
appropriate use of, 91–93, 104, 106
and overeager children, 168
and technology, 188, 205

Imbalance of power, 172
Immediate goals, 63, 68. *See also*
Short-term goals
Immediate gratification, 112–114
Impulsivity, 88, 89, 139
Independence
as cultural value, 4
definitions of, 11–14
elements of, 12
pseudo-, 26–28
Independent children, 9–32. *See also
specific headings*
across developmental stages, 14–23
challenges with, 9
and defining independence, 11–14
and guiding with questions, 23–24

Independent children (*continued*)
struggles as important experiences
of, 31–32
support for, 25–29
and talking with your child, 29–31
Independent technology use. *See*
Technology
Infants
behaviors of, 119
communicating love to, 103
games played by, 151
and helicopter parenting, 28
needs of, 25, 103
Insecurity, 51–52
Intellectual property, 182
Internet, 179
Intimidation, 146–147

Kinesthetic learning style, 78

Ladder visualization, 63, 65, 85
Late adolescence, 19–22
Learning differences, 224–227
Learning disabilities, 224–227
Learning styles, 78–80
*Learning to Slow Down and Pay
Attention* (Nadeau, Dixon, &
Bey), 220
Listening, 51, 90
The Little Engine That Could (Watty
Piper), 33
Long-term goals, 62–64, 86
Loss, 211–215
Loving, 52–54, 116–117

Marshmallow Test study, 112–113
Mayo Clinic, 218
Medication, 223
Mischel, Walter, 113
Mistakes, 144–146
Modeling
of communication skills, 21
of frustration tolerance, 123

of self-monitoring, 141–144
of social graces, 155
of strategies for calming down, 89
Moderation, 134–138
Motivation
and curiosity, 77–78
self-, 71–73
Music, 111

Negative bystanders, 176
Negative self-talk, 87
Neutral bystanders, 176
Newton, Isaac, 71
Nonjudgmental communication, 145

Obsessive–compulsive disorder (OCD),
75
Online education, 179
Options, 79, 81, 82, 83, 95, 97, 112,
143, 153, 166
Organize, 57, 59, 61, 69, 74, 75, 78,
109, 150, 182, 183
Overeagerness, 167–168
Overprotection, 115

Pain, emotional, 114–116
Parental controls, 201
Parenting skills, 3–4
Parenting styles, 5
Patience, 102–103. *See also* Frustration
tolerance
Peer pressure, 128, 130–134, 231
Perpetrator, 196
Perseverance, 39, 73–75
Perseveration, 73–75
Physical disabilities, 224–227
Physical punishment, 146–147
Physical touch, 52
Piaget, Jean, 142
Piper, Watty, 33
Plagiarism, 182
Play dates, 62, 110, 171, 228
Play time, 70, 236–237

Politeness, 153–157
Popular parent, 107, 116–117
Positive bystanders, 175–176
Positive self-talk, 87–88, 110–111
Praise, 72
Pride, 129
Prioritization, 69–71
Problem solving, 81, 82–83, 85, 144,
    171
Protection, of children, 114–115
Pseudoindependence, 26–28
Punishment, 144, 146–147

Quality time, 52
Questions
    guidance with, 23–24, 65–67
    and self-monitoring, 145
Quiet reasoning, 104

Race, 219–220
Realistic goals, 64–68
Rebellion, 131, 138, 146
Religion, 213, 220
Rituals, 212, 213
Robotics, 179
Role-playing, 93–95, 131, 172
Rolling Stones, 111

Sadness, 16, 214, 215
Safety, 166
Sarcasm, 106, 157, 196
Schedules, 70, 216, 217
School
    frustration tolerance in, 113
    and technology, 180–184, 189–193
Self-consequences, 147–150
Self-doubt, 33, 36, 37
Self-monitoring, 125–150
    and acceptance of consequences,
        147–150
    and child's image, 127–130
    definitions of, 126–127
    and intimidation, 146–147

and learning from mistakes, 144–146
modeling of, 141–144
and moderation, 134–138
and peer pressure, 130–134
and presence of parent, 138–141
putting in effort for helping child
    with, 232
and technology, 202–203
Self-motivation, 71–73
Self-reliance, 12, 73
Self-talk
    negative, 87
    positive, 87–88, 110–111
Separation, 215–217
Short-term goals, 62–64, 68, 76, 86, 99
Shyness, 227–229
Skype, 181, 186
Social competence, 6, 150, 151, 152,
    155
Social graces, 153–157
Socialization, 184–188, 232
Social media, 131–132, 188–194
Social rejection, 169–171
Social skills, 151–178
    and body language, 157–167
    and bullying, 171–178
    and communication, 152–153
    and politeness, 153–157
    and social rejection, 169–171
    and trying too hard, 167–168
    and verbal intonations, 157–159
Special circumstances, 209–230
    attention paid to, 229
    and healthy coping, 211–220
    personal challenges as, 220–229
Specialness, 119–120
Spell-check, 191
Step-by-step thinking, 85
Stepchildren, 218–220
Stranger danger, 199, 201
Strengths, 12
Struggles, 31–32
Success, 37–39

Support
  for independent children, 25–29
  offering consistent and daily,
    54–55
  and special circumstances, 209
Swift, Taylor, 111

Target, 172, 173, 175, 178, 195, 197
Teachable moments, 70, 81, 103
Teasing, 128, 172
Technology, 179–207
  in children's social lives, 184–188
  at home, 193–194
  monitoring child's use of, 194–204
  and school, 180–184, 189–193
  taking breaks from, 204–206
Teenagers
  decision making by, 89–96
  independent steps taken by, 19
  needs of, 103
  physical presentation of, 163–164
  self-monitoring of, 138
Temper tantrums
  and calming down, 88
  as common occurrence with toddlers,
    16
  responding to, 120–123
Terrible twos, 14, 83
Texting, 179, 184–185

Thinking tasks, 88
Time management, 69–71
Toddlers
  communication styles of, 109,
    120–121
  decision making by, 83–84
  independent actions of, 14–17
  needs of, 103
Tolerance, 223
Toys, 110, 206
TV shows, 131, 157, 162

Unconditional love, 116–117
Unintentional bullying, 171
Unrealistic goals, 64–65
Upstanders, 175–176

Verbal intonations, 52, 157–159, 205
Victim, 173, 195, 197
Video games, 110, 186, 188, 193, 199
Visual learning style, 78

Waiting, 102–103
Weaknesses, 12
"What Would You Do?" game, 76,
  96–97
Word processors, 191

Zen Buddhism, 31

ABOUT THE AUTHORS

Wendy L. Moss, PhD, ABPP, is a licensed clinical psychologist and a certified school psychologist. She has worked with children, tweens, teens, parents, and educators and has collaborated with other mental health colleagues. She has worked in school, hospital, clinic, residential treatment, and private practice settings. Dr. Moss has counseled children as young as 3 and realizes that even such young children are capable of starting their journey toward independence.

Dr. Moss also teaches groups of children on a variety of topics ranging from social competence to mindfulness to becoming an "upstander." Through her book *Children Don't Come With an Instruction Manual: A Teacher's Guide to Problems That Affect Learners*, Dr. Moss has helped teachers understand the behaviors and emotions of children in the classroom. She has also authored or coauthored a variety of books for children (e.g., *Being Me: A Kid's Guide to Boosting Confidence and Self-Esteem*; *Bounce Back: How to Be a Resilient Kid*; *The Tween Book: A Growing-Up Guide for the Changing You* [coauthored with Donald A. Moses, MD]; *The Survival Guide for Kids With Physical Disabilities and Challenges* [coauthored with Susan A. Taddonio, DPT]; *School Made Easier: A Kid's Guide to Study Strategies and Anxiety-Busting Tools* [coauthored with Robin A. DeLuca-Acconi, LCSW]; *The Survival Guide for Kids in Special*

Education (and Their Parents): Understanding What Special Ed Is and How It Can Help You [coauthored with Denise M. Campbell, MS]). In addition, Dr. Moss is a Diplomate in School Psychology through the American Board of Professional Psychology and has been appointed as a Fellow of the American Academy of School Psychology.

Donald A. Moses, MD, is a psychiatrist who specializes in the treatment of adolescents and young adults. He has many years of experience in treating patients with psychoanalytic and psychodynamic psychotherapy, which has given him a clear understanding of the importance of children developing particular skills so that they later can be functional adults rather than resort to self-destructive behavior and difficulty functioning.

Dr. Moses gained his experience while working in psychiatric hospitals, as a psychiatric consultant to adolescent substance abuse treatment programs, as a flight medical officer in the United States Air Force, and from many years in private practice. His first book was *Are You Driving Your Children to Drink? Coping With Teenage Alcohol and Drug Abuse* (coauthored with Robert E. Burger). It highlights the essential need for parents to be there for their children, providing a sense of love and security throughout their childhood and teenage years. More recently, Dr. Moses coauthored with Wendy L. Moss, PhD, *The Tween Book: A Growing Up Guide for the Changing You.* He has lectured to high school and college students, has spoken with educators as well as with parent audiences, and has spoken on radio and television on the topic of parent–child relationships.